THE
YORKSHIRE TERRIER
TODAY

Veronica Sameja-Hilliard

Howell Book House

New York

HOWELL BOOK HOUSE
IDG Books Worldwide, Inc.
An International Data Group Company
Foster City, CA • Chicago, IL • Indianapolis, IN • New York, NY • Southlake, TX

ISBN 1-58245-167-2

Library of Congress Cataloging-in-Publication Data
available on request

Manufactured in Singapore

10 9 8 7 6 5 4 3 2 1

ACKNOWLEDGEMENTS

Many thanks to all the Yorkie folk who have given me so much information about their own dogs and supplied me with photographs. Special thanks to Osman Sameja and also to my son, Adam, for his patience in teaching me how to work the computer. Without his help, this book would never have been finished.

Verolian The Governess.
Photo: Amanda Bulbeck.

Contents

1

INTRODUCING THE YORKSHIRE TERRIER

There is nothing more beautiful and rewarding than a Yorkie, with his gleaming coat and sassy walk: he is a joy to watch and a joy to own. Loyalty, devotion, and a zest for life are all part and parcel of this little dog.

"Beautiful to look at, active as a kitten, vivacious as the most 'perky Pom', the Yorkshire Terrier is the acme of Toydog virtue and perfection, looked at from every angle." So wrote Theo Marples, the originator and editor of the UK canine newspaper *Our Dogs*, in his first edition of *Show Dogs*. Not so the Hon. Mrs Neville Lytton, who wrote in 1911: "As for the unfortunate show Yorkshire Terrier with his unnatural existence as a 'clothes peg', the less said the better." Clearly, she was of the opinion that little would be said about this dog in the future.

How wrong she was! This man-made creation of the 19th century is truly the modern dog. Adapting to all walks of life – country or town, cottage or castle – the Yorkie lives in them all with great satisfaction. Prepared to walk miles with his owner or just be the house dog, he is also content with exercising himself in his garden and running around the house. A life-expectancy of up to 15 years makes this little dog an excellent long-term companion. He has a friendly disposition and a cheerful personality. Easy to train and agreeable to all, he makes a fine partner for most people.

His diminutive size means the Yorkie is fairly inexpensive to keep – though he imagines himself to be much larger than he actually is. His size is very convenient and often allows him privileges that larger dogs sometimes do not have. For example, I have often stayed in hotels where dogs are not allowed, and have been allowed to take my Yorkies in once the staff have seen the size of the dogs.

The fact the Yorkie does not shed his coat may also appeal to you – especially

OPPOSITE PAGE: Ch. Phalbrienz Tamarix: Top Toy in the UK, 1992. The gleaming coat and zest for life are among the many attractions of the Yorkshire Terrier.

if members of your family suffer from allergies.

COLOURFUL CHARACTERS

The first Yorkie I bought, with money borrowed from my father, was Mitzi. She won the hearts of everyone she met and was my constant companion for 13 years. My darling Mitzi was the true Yorkshire character, her humour and devotion unfailing.

When I owned a pet shop, people would come in just to meet Mitzi. On one occasion, a gentleman came in and told me he had no love for dogs but had heard of her and would like to own her. I explained that she was not for sale at any price, and he became a regular

visitor. Strangely enough, he had no interest in any other dog – only the extrovert Mitzi.

Over the years, she attracted many admirers. She was very discriminating in her friends, so I always had my heart in my mouth when she met someone new. She would either promptly snap at them, or fall in love and be their friend for life. She was a loving, loyal companion, who brought me so much pleasure in her short life.

One of my girls, Sylvia, has surprised us all. Before her, not one of the Yorkies I have owned has ever caught or remotely shown any interest in vermin, which caused me to doubt their origins as rat-catchers. Sylvia actually catches mice! The awful part is that she will devour them if you're not quick enough to retrieve them.

The terrier nature is never more apparent than in the Yorkie's need to dig. All my dogs are great gardeners, digging up plants as soon as I plant them. At present, I have many hole-diggers. My Ch. Verolian Out of the Blue can dig a hole as well as any gopher.

PEOPLE DOGS

COMPANION DOGS

For the person living alone, a Yorkshire Terrier will provide companionship, play, and a sense of being needed. An understanding and loving companion, he is an expert in dispelling loneliness,

The typical terrier temperament is never far from the surface.
Photo: Russell Fine Art.

relaxing his owners, and making them laugh.

As well as providing companionship, the Yorkshire Terrier has a great need to receive human companionship, and hates being ignored. I'm sure this trait comes from the breed's early history as a companion.

He does not take kindly to being left for long periods of time, which is natural in any dog. It is not only cruel to leave a dog alone for a considerable period of time, it is also likely to turn your Yorkie into an antisocial hooligan who will chew your house to pieces. If you do have to leave your Yorkie for more than three hours, make arrangements for a friend to pop in to let him out and feed him.

Left alone for a few hours, he will usually sleep. If you leave your Yorkie regularly at the same time and for the same length of time, he will quickly adapt to your routine. You may like to consider getting your dog a friend to keep him company when left alone. Two Yorkies can get on very well together, if introduced properly. I find a year gap between them ideal since the first Yorkie will have established himself in the family and is likely to welcome his new friend with great enthusiasm. Two pups from the same litter can become deadly enemies as they often vie with each other to become pack leader.

THERAPY DOGS

Because of their love of people, Yorkies make perfect therapy dogs. Therapy dogs visit people in hospitals, residential homes and schools, providing companionship to those who may not usually have access to a pet. More than 130 have registered with Pets As Therapy in the UK.

Therapeutic is perhaps not the first word that springs to mind regarding a Yorkie but, to the sick and elderly, the act of stroking a friendly, living dog decreases stress and gives a feeling of well-being, and the Yorkie is the ideal dog for this. He loves to be touched and adored, and is well-suited to being the centre of attention.

Many Yorkies are registered therapy dogs in America, too, and hold the title

The typical terrier temperament is never far from the surface.
Photo: Russell Fine Art.

Polo, owned by Joan Young, works as a therapy dog.

Cosette: A remarkable Yorkie who has saved her owner's life.

of TDI (Therapy Dogs International). These dogs and their owners make regular visits to nursing homes, assisted living facilities, schools and retirement homes. The Yorkies enjoy making the visits as much as, if not more than, the persons they are visiting.

ASSISTANCE DOGS

Meet 'Cosette' a tiny 2 lb Yorkie Service Dog owned by DebbieLynn, Beverly Hills, California. Debbie was severely injured several years ago in an automobile accident which left her with some debilitating after-effects. She needed a service dog to be able to maintain her independence, but was told that she would not be able to lift anything over 3 lbs. After months of searching she finally found a Yorkie puppy that would be tiny as an adult. The Delta Society referred her to a trainer of special needs dogs and thus little Cosette's training was begun.

Cosette can dial 911 (the universal telephone number in the US for emergency), she can also dial DebbieLynn's mother. She can detect changes in DebbieLynn's heart rate or skipped beats and can let DebbieLynn know which one it is. Cosette has taught herself to find the pressure point to stop bleeding, as one of DebbieLynn's problems is a rare blood disorder. She can also warn DebbieLynn of an oncoming migraine in time for DebbieLynn to take the necessary medication. Cosette also can alert DebbieLynn to someone at the door, to the microwave or to the dryer bell.

Cosette is a remarkable little Yorkie and thus far has saved her owner's life seven times.

FAMILY PET

The way your family lives will decide the character of your Yorkshire Terrier. A noisy, boisterous family will have a noisy, boisterous dog. A quiet family

Family lifestyle will influence the way your dog's character develops.
Photo: Amanda Bulbeck.

will have a calm dog. Most Yorkies are not suited to noisy households as they can be overwhelmed by the excitement and may develop a nervous temperament as a result.

Yorkies themselves are not the quietest of dogs, nor are they the yappy dogs many people believe them to be. Yes, they will be attentive to strange noises and the knock on the door – barking like a Rottweiler – but this can be an asset to any home.

A Yorkie supplies companionship, fun and relaxation for the whole family, especially children. You should be careful with young children, however, as they can be clumsy. In fact, many breeders will not even consider selling a puppy to a young family, since the pup may easily be damaged, causing serious injury to a fine-boned dog.

Young children must be taught to respect the little dog, and not to overtire him or treat him as a toy. Always encourage children to sit on the floor with a pup, and to be gentle. There is always a possibility that a Yorkie can be dropped if a child stands up with a pup in his arms.

A dog-child relationship can be very special and no child should be denied it. Encourage any children in the house to become involved in grooming, feeding and exercising their new pet – all under your supervision, of course. The child will then grow up having learnt the responsibilities of caring for a pet.

CAT COMPANION

It is not a daunting proposition to have cats and Yorkies together – in fact, they can live in harmony together if they are introduced to each other properly.

The arrival of a kitten can be a very exciting time, and the dog soon picks up on the family mood and becomes excited too. Make sure your Yorkie is calm before placing the kitten on the floor. Your dog must be restrained so that he cannot chase, play or scare the

The vigilant Yorkshire Terrier makes a surprisingly good guard. 'Misha' by Vavra Photography.

Canine companions (left to right): Aust. Ch. Deebees Dionysius (sire), Aust. Ch. Karojenbe Temptation (daughter), and Karojenbe Itanda Bit (son). Photo: Animal Pics.

new cat. Allow them to sniff each other. If the dog oversteps the mark and intimidates the cat, she is likely to arch her back and fluff her fur up, giving the impression she is much larger than she actually is. Cats usually become the boss in most households, and it will not be long before your Yorkie learns the rules and treats your cat with respect.

Some Yorkies are likely to ignore the cat's existence after the initial introductions, but some will become firm friends with their new companion. Many adore cats and will seek her out to snuggle up to her soft fur coat. Being heat-lovers, Yorkies usually quickly discover that the cat is an excellent source of warmth.

I have had two cats with Yorkies, and they have mothered the dogs, washing their faces and accompanying them on country walks.

The adaptable Yorkie will take on board all members of the family – including this Cockatiel – as long as introductions are carefully supervised. Photo: Carol Ann Johnson.

CANINE FRIENDS

I would rather introduce a cat to a Yorkie than introduce a strange dog, especially if the dog is larger. I personally would never let a large, young, boisterous dog loose with my Yorkies, in case of a mishap. A quick knock can easily concuss a tiny dog.

If the occasion arises and you have to

introduce a new dog to the household, do be cautious. If the strange dog approaches your dog with his tail up and wagging, they will probably become friends. If, however, the newcomer keeps his body rigid, and his tail stiff, you should monitor them particularly closely, as it could result in a dog fight.

A large dog coming into the house can really upset the apple cart. Your Yorkie will not realise he is so small and will regard himself a fair match for the 'intruder'. If he feels his territory is threatened, most Yorkies will not hesitate to attack.

The best way to introduce new dogs is on neutral ground so that neither feels territorial. If the newcomer is a large dog, keep him on a lead so that you have control over him. They can then sniff each other safely, and, hopefully, will become friends.

VISITORS

Yorkies usually greet visitors with great enthusiasm, especially if they know them. Dog lovers, old or new, are always welcomed with a warm bark, and a frantic tail wag. You can see the

Loyal, affectionate and courageous – dog to be proud of.

pleasure in their eyes. They will also be hopeful that tea and cakes will be on offer. Yorkies may be small, but they can be very agile when cakes are on the menu. My Justine would leap on to the kitchen chair and then on to the table to get to any goodies left there. Being the unselfish soul she is, she always makes sure the others get their share, by dropping it over the edge of the table to the expectant gang below!

When strangers visit, make sure your Yorkie is put in another room until the visitor has settled. You can then allow him in to introduce himself. This enables both guest and dog to meet in a calm and controlled manner.

2 ORIGINS OF THE YORKSHIRE TERRIER

an's association with the dog is thousands of years old, stretching from when the dog first came into man's affection as a hunter and companion, to the present day. The human fascination for breeding and adapting gradually brought about the many breeds of dog in existence today – all there to do a job, not least to be man's best friend. The Yorkshire Terrier is no exception: a creation entirely man-made – from various breeds – to suit a purpose, probably as both ratter and household pet.

CONTRIBUTORY BREEDS

In the late 18th century, apart from a few turnpikes, roads were impassable to heavy traffic in the winter as they became mud baths. In Yorkshire and Lancashire the only routes for goods and passengers were the canals. Water being the only source of power for the factories and mills, sites along the canals

were at a premium. The advent of steam soon altered this: factories and mills would now be built at any convenient point along the railway. Many of the engineers who came to Yorkshire were from Scotland, where the main engine works were, and they were encouraged to stay.

During the Industrial Revolution, many other Scots would have made the exodus from their native Scotland to the Yorkshire Ridings, seeking work in the mines and mills. All these families would have brought their native dogs with them, that would certainly have included the Skye Terrier, Paisley Terrier, and Clydesdale Terrier – all of which contributed to the Yorkshire Terrier.

In Hutchinson's *Dog Encyclopedia* (1935), we find the following:

The Paisley breeders were mostly weavers and they were adept in benching their Clydesdales in perfect bloom. The dogs lay

'A Terrier in an Interior'.
W.J. Chapman, 1861.
Photo: Iona Antiques.

*beside their owners [and all the free time
they] had they were brushing and keeping
their terriers in order. In this way it was
impossible for the dogs' coats to become
matted or destroyed.*

In fact, the oil from the wool they
worked – lanolin – would have
protected and conditioned the coats.
Since lanolin is very oily, the dogs also
played the role of 'towel', invaluable for
keeping their owners' hands dry.

SKYE TERRIER

This breed has been in existence for
many centuries. Four hundred years
ago, Dr John Caius, Master of Gonville
and Caius College, Cambridge
University, and Court Physician to
Edward VI, Queen Mary and Queen
Elizabeth I, wrote:

*A cur brought out the barbarous borders
fro' the uttermost countryes northward
which by reason of the length of heare
makes showe neither of face nor body.*

We can assume this dog was probably a
Skye. It most probably carried the
blood of the Maltese, Mediterranean
Toy terriers that were almost certainly
washed ashore from the Armada ships
that sank around the Scottish Coast
after the Spanish defeat in 1588. In
Scotland and the Isles especially, the
terrier's job would have been the
destruction of foxes, badgers, martens
and even wild cats, which meant
burrowing, digging and fighting in
confined spaces. It also demanded
powerful jaws, which can still be found
today beneath the Skye's abundant
whiskers. These dogs were large, 8.3kg
(18lb) and over, and their coats harsh
and of reasonable length. Colouring
would have varied, including blue-and-
tan, grizzle and wheaten.

CLYDESDALE TERRIER AND PAISLEY TERRIER

Initially, the Clydesdale Terrier and the
Paisley Terrier were two separate breeds.
The Clydesdale, a blue and tan terrier,
weighed up to 18 lbs, and the Paisley, a
blue and light blue terrier, weighed up
to 12 lbs. These silky-coated dogs could
possibly have been the result of soft-
coated Skye Terriers, so disliked by true
Skye breeders. The silky coat would
have certainly attracted admirers and, as
we shall see, there was a move to show
the soft-coated Skye offspring.

Interestingly, many Clydesdale breeders also bred the Skye Terriers. Which of these two breeds came first is anyone's guess, but they did eventually become the same breed adopting the name of the Clydesdale, who won over with his colour whereas the Paisley won with his size. Let us assume these were the foundation for the Yorkshire Terrier.

By the time of the first Crufts show in 1891, the Clydesdale was a rare variety, and it was extinct by the end of the First World War. Blythswood Peace (Lorne O'Donne ex Blythswood Queen) was Best Of Breed (BOB) in 1894 and 1895. Bred by Mr T. Eskine, she was born in 1890. Six Clydesdale Terriers were entered in 1895.

Clydesdale breeder Mr George Shaw wrote of the breed:

The Clydesdale when taken care of is a very useful house dog and good at vermin. He is easily carried in the arms, as his weight should not exceed 18lb. When clean and well groomed he is a pretty animal, and is much healthier than most breeds.

I will now mention a few show dogs which were on the bench and did a bit of winning. These three or four dogs were all the same stamp and weight. First we had Lorne O'Donne, next Blythswood Pearl who was a picture to look at. Last we had Ch. Ballochmyle Wee Wattie and Strad, who are about the one type and weight, and are both pretty Terriers. There are some judges who do not know the breed and weight and place the dogs wrong. A Clydesdale Terrier is a Fancy Terrier, and quite different from the Skye Terrier, both in type and quality. The Skye is a much more weighty and coarser dog, and the coat, of course, is quite different!

There were two clubs initially: the Clydesdale Club and the Skye and Clydesdale Club, but they did not prevent the breed's extinction. There

Paisley Terrier.

Clydesdale Terrier:
'Ch. Ballochmyle Wee Wattie'.

Mr John King's Paisley (or Clydesdale) Terrier – 'Lorne of Paisley'.

A Paisley (Clydesdale) Terrier, 1880.

were only ever four Champions.

The first Clydesdale Terrier Champion was Ch. Ballochmyle Wee Wattie (Roy ex Fly), bred by Mr Williams and born in 1900. He was BOB at Crufts in 1905 when there were no Challenge Certificates (CCs) on offer for the breed.

The second Champion was Ch. Ballochmyle Saucy, who won the only CC on offer for BOB winner at Crufts, in both 1903 and 1904. The Championship Prizes and Championship Certificates that were on offer in previous years were similar to the UK CC system, but, for the less popular breeds, a pair was not on offer at every Championship show.

The third Clydesdale Champion was Mr Shaw's Ch. Carmen, who was BOB in 1914, the last year the breed was classified at Crufts.

The last Champion was Ch. Craigneuk (Rutherglen Provast ex Molly), who was BOB in 1911 (the year she gained her title) and 1912. She was born in 1907.

In his book, *Dogs of Scotland*, published in 1887 and 1891, Mr D.J. Thomson-Gray tells us a great deal about the Paisley or Clydesdale Terrier, sometimes called the Silky-coated Skye Terrier.

Unlike its contemporaries, the Skye and Scots Terrier – whose origin dates so far back that it is lost in the mists of antiquity – the history of the lovely house pet, the Paisley Terrier, is easily traced, although the precise date when it first appeared cannot be fixed – for this reason, that up to a recent date they were exhibited and won prizes at West of Scotland Shows as Skye Terriers.

These dogs, while possessing all the characteristics of the Skye, as far as form, colour and length of coat is concerned, have a soft silky coat, and on this account have been known for the past ten years or so as Glasgow or Paisley Terriers. Previous to this, however, they were simply known as Skyes, and exhibited as such. The Paisley Terrier has never been very widely distributed, and very seldom found beyond the Valley of the Clyde. At the shows which used to be held at Glasgow half a dozen or more years back, these silky-coated terriers were seen in all their beauty, and the fact of their appearing there as Skyes was what first brought them into prominence.

The fanciers of the hard-coated Skyes rose in arms against them, holding that they were not Skyes, as they had a silky coat, and were only pretty 'mongrels' bred from Skye Terrier 'rejections' and ought to be known as Glasgow or Paisley Skyes. On the other hand, the breeders of the silky-coated dogs held, as a matter of course, that the texture of the coats their dogs possessed was the correct one. This was untenable, as, until the introduction of the breed, no Scottish dog had a silky or soft coat. No good feeling existed between the rivals, and the storm which had been brewing culminated in a great paper war which ended in favour of the hard coats. Thus it was settled and agreed upon that the Skye Terrier should have a hard coat.

As a result of this decision, interest in the silky-coated dogs began to wane. However, a few breeders kept the breed going, through sheer love of the dogs. They formed a club and changed the name from Paisley to Clydesdale Terrier.

THE EARLY YORKIE AND ITS ANCESTORS

The Breed Standard for the Paisley-turned-Clydesdale was first drawn up in 1891 and again in 1896. A standard for a Paisley Terrier can be found in *The Complete Book of the Dog*, by Robert Leighten. He lists it under Clydesdale, but it is obviously different. If we look at it, we can see many similarities to the original Yorkshire Terrier Standard of the Yorkshire Terrier Club. I will put all of them together for comparison.

Head

Clydesdale, 1891 – Long, flat and massive, with good stout muzzle and strong jaws. Teeth must be perfectly level, over- or under-shot are faults, under-shot the greater of the two.

Clydesdale, 1896 – The skull, which is slightly domed, should be very narrow between the ears, gradually widening towards the eyes, and tapering very slightly to the nose. It should be covered with long silky hair perfectly straight, without any appearance of curl or waviness, and extending well beyond the nose. It should be particularly plentiful on the sides of the head, where it is joined by that from the ears, giving the head a very large and rather heavy appearance in proportion to the size of the dog. The muzzle should be very deep and powerful, tapering very slightly to the nose, which should be large and well spread over the muzzle and must always be black. The jaws should be strong, with the teeth perfectly level.

Paisley – Fairly long skull, flat and very narrow between the ears, gradually widening towards the eyes and tapering very slightly to the nose, which must be black, the jaws strong and the teeth level.

Yorkshire Terrier – Should be rather small and flat, not too prominent or round in the skull, nor too long in the muzzle, with a perfect black nose. The fall on the head to be long, of a rich golden tan, deep in colour at the sides of the head about the ear roots, and on the muzzle where it should be very long. The hair on the chest a rich bright tan. On no account must the tan on the head extend on to the neck, nor must there be any sooty or dark hair intermingled with any of the tan.

Ears
Clydesdale, 1891 – Ears, as in Skyes, are set on high and invariably pricked, standing quite straight, and not falling to the side, covered with long hair, and nicely fringed, the latter an important point.

Clydesdale, 1896 – This is a most important point in this breed. They should be as small as possible, set on high, and carried perfectly erect. They should be covered with long silky hair, which should hang in a beautiful fringe down the sides of the head, joining that on the jaws. (Well carried, finely fringed ears is one of the greatest points of

beauty in the breed, as it is also one of the most difficult to obtain.) A badly carried and poorly feathered ear is a serious fault in a Clydesdale Terrier.

Paisley – Small, set very high on the top of the head, carried perfectly erect, and covered with long silky hair hanging in a heavy fringe down the sides of the head.

Yorkshire – Small, V-shaped, and carried semi-erect, or erect, and not far apart, covered with short hair, colour to be of a deep rich tan.

Eyes
Clydesdale, 1891 – Eyes, which are obscured by hair, dark brown of a good size, but not prominent.

Clydesdale, 1896 – The eyes should be rather wide apart. They should be large, round, moderately full, but not prominent; expressive of great intelligence and in colour, various shades of brown.

Paisley – Medium in size, dark in colour, not prominent, but having a sharp terrier-like expression; eyelids black.

Yorkshire – Medium dark and sparkling, having a sharp intelligent expression, and placed so as to look directly forward. They should not be prominent and the edge of the eyelids should be of a dark colour.

Body

Clydesdale, 1891 – Long, perfectly straight in the back, wide at the ribs and well ribbed home, must not be flat-sided or tucked up in the flank; the loins broad and well covered with muscle.

Clydesdale, 1896 – The body should be very long, deep in chest and well ribbed up; the back perfectly level, not sloping from the loins to shoulder as in the Dandie.

Paisley – Long, deep in chest, well ribbed up, back being perfectly level.

Yorkshire – Very compact, and a good loin. Level on the top of the back.

Legs and feet

Clydesdale, 1891 – Forelegs short, muscular, and perfectly straight, well set on under the body; hindlegs, short and straight. The dog should stand fair on his legs and feet, which are of fair size, pointing straight to the front.

Clydesdale, 1896 – The legs should be short and straight as possible, and well set under the body, both legs and feet with well-covered silky hair and in a good specimen the legs are scarcely seen, as they are almost hidden by the coat.

Paisley – Legs as short and straight as possible, well set under the body, and entirely covered with silky hair. Feet round and cat-like.

Yorkshire – Legs (under forequarters) quite straight, well covered with hair of a rich golden tan a few shades lighter at the ends than at the roots, not extending higher on the forelegs than the elbow.

Tail

Clydesdale, 1891 – Carried in a straight line with the back, when not excited; free from twist or curl, and having a nice thin fringe of hair hanging from it.

Clydesdale, 1896 – Should be perfectly straight, not too long, and carried almost level with the back; it must be nicely fringed or feathered.

Paisley – Perfectly straight, carried almost level with the back, and heavily feathered.

Yorkshire – Originally carried five points for its carriage. Customarily docked to medium length with plenty of hair, carried a little higher than the level of the back.

Colour

Clydesdale, 1891 – A level, bright steel blue, extending from the back of the head to the root of the tail, and on no account intermingled with any fawn, light or dark hairs. The head, legs and feet should be a clear, bright golden tan, free from grey, sooty or dark hairs. The tail should be very dark blue or black.

Clydesdale, 1896 – The colours range from dark blue to light fawn; but those most desired are the various shades of blue – dark blue for preference, but without any approach to blackness or sootiness. The colour of the head should be a beautiful silvery blue, which gets darker on the ears; the back various shades of dark blue, inclining to silver on the lower parts of the body and legs. The tail is generally the same shade or a little darker than the back.

Paisley – Various shades of blue – dark blue for preference. The hair on head and lower extremities slightly lighter than the body above, but it should not approach a linty [fawn] shade.

Yorkshire – A dark steel blue (not silver blue), extending from the occiput to the root of tail, and on no account mingled with fawn, bronze or dark hairs. The hair on the chest a rich bright tan. All tan hair should be darker at the roots than in the middle, shading to a still lighter tan at the tips.

Coat

Clydesdale, 1891 – Long, flat and free from curl – very soft and silky in texture. The longer and finer the hair the more value is attached to it. The hair, parted at the shoulder and continued to set-on at tail, should hang gracefully from the body, and cover the head and eyes, and reach to the nose.

Clydesdale, 1896 – Should be very long, perfectly straight, and free from any trace of curl or waviness; very glossy and silky in texture (not linty) and should be without any of the piley undercoat found in the Skye Terrier.

Paisley – As long and straight as possible, free from all trace of curl or waviness, very glossy and silky in texture, with an entire absence of undercoat.

Yorkshire – The hair on the body moderately long and perfectly straight (not wavy), glossy, like silk, and of a fine silk texture.

General Appearance

Clydesdale, 1891 – A long, low, stoutly built terrier, with an intelligent expression or countenance, and a long flowing flat-lying straight coat.

Clydesdale, 1896 – That of a long low dog, having a rather large head in proportion to its size, and with a coat which looks like silk or spun glass. It shows considerably more style or quality than almost any other fancy terrier.

Paisley – A long, low, level dog with heavily fringed erect ears, and a long coat like the finest silk or spun glass which hangs quite straight and evenly down each side from a parting extending from the nose to the root of the tail.

Yorkshire – Should be that of a long-coated toy terrier, the coat hanging quite straight and evenly down each side, a parting extending from the nose to end of the tail. The animal should be very compact and neat, the carriage being very upright, and having an important air. The general outline should convey the existence of a vigorous and well-proportioned body.

As to weight, it would appear that the Clydesdale could weigh 16-18lb (7.3–8.2kg), whereas the Paisley could not exceed 12lb (5.4kg) and was referred to as the only 'Toy Dog' produced by Scotland. Nowadays, the show Yorkshire must not exceed 7lb (3.1kg) in weight.

It is interesting that the Clydesdale Breed Standard 1896, mentions the Dandie Dinmont when giving details on the body. Why this dog should even be mentioned is a puzzle. It has been suggested that the Dandie Dinmont played a role in the creation of the Silken Terriers, but no evidence to support this has been found, so why mention it? It could explain some of the strange toplines we can still see today!

The Breed Standards suggest that the Paisley/Clydesdale is a descendant from the silky-coated Skyes. As to which came first, the Clydesdale or the Paisley, we can never be certain. Since there appears to have been this concentrated effort to blend the names, this question is probably unanswerable.

In *The Book of the Dog* by Brian Vesey-Fitzgerald, published in the US in 1948, we find the following in the section 'Clydesdale or Paisley Terrier':

This breed no longer appears in the Kennel Stud Book. But it is not extinct, though its hey-day is far past. It is a very old breed, just how old no-one knows, and it is probably the ancestor of both the Skye Terrier and the Yorkshire Terrier. In this connection I have heard it said it was produced by crossing the Yorkshire with the Skye; this is nonsense. The Yorkshire Terrier is comparatively a new breed, the Clydesdale was in its hey-day before 1855: indeed, well before that date, since in 1856 it was regarded as in danger of extinction and there was a powerful movement to put it on its feet again.

The Clydesdale Terrier Club was formed in 1887, and in the following year the Kennel Club classified it in their stud book. The Clydesdale Terrier Club did not last long and was succeeded by the Paisley Terrier Club, which I believe still exists, though it has long since ceased to be a specialist club and has become a general canine society.

OTHER LOCAL TERRIERS

Let us assume that the Clydesdale was the basic foundation for the Yorkshire Terrier. We know it was the Scottish emigrants who brought the Scotch Terrier to Yorkshire, and we must not forget that all the Scottish terriers were hard-coated apart from the Paisley/Clydesdale. However, in their new country, there would have been local-bred dogs ready to mix their blood with their new neighbours and create a crude Yorkshire Terrier.

One of these could possibly have been the Waterside Terrier, a small dog varying from 2.7–9.1kg (6–20lb) in weight, and with a long coat, blue-coloured head and grizzle-coloured body coat. These little terriers were keen ratters and probably helped their owners in poaching. Willing to please, they would have made excellent family pets. In an attempt to prevent their farm or estate workers from poaching, the rich landowners of this time – the 19th Century – did not allow them to have large dogs, but small dogs were permitted. Knowing the Yorkie of today, I'm sure this little chap was as game as any big dog.

Since the railways had opened up new horizons, the Manchester Terrier would surely have been introduced, perhaps for its black-and-tan markings. As to the final ingredients to produce our Yorkshire Terrier, only those canny old Yorkshire breeders really know.

We must realise, too, that these little dogs, even in their early days of development, were very sociable, living and working in close proximity with people. The weavers' dogs would have been crossed with local dogs, introducing new traits and probably reducing the size, according to individual requirements – probably a ratter by night and a companion at work and play during the day. It would not have taken the Yorkshire breeders long to realise the potential of these glamorous little ratters as pets for Victorian Londoners. I am sure the breed's life as a ratter was very short: soon dogs with quality coats were being bred solely as domestic companions. Soon a crude prototype of the Yorkshire Terrier emerged, still known for the moment as the Scotch Terrier.

THE YORKSHIRE TERRIER EMERGES

By the 1850s, dogs were being exhibited at shows. Many of these would have been haphazard affairs, often held in public houses. Yorkshire or Scotch Terriers were shown in various classes as Toy Terriers, Broken-haired Scotch, Scotch Terriers, Blue and Fawn Terriers, and Yorkshire Terriers. This must have been very confusing for the judges since, as a single dog could go into so many varying classes, it did! They had weight limits too, so a Yorkshire could have been anything

from 2.3–8.2kg (5–18lb). No doubt the original Yorkie could have been shown as a Paisley or Clydesdale, and probably would have got away with it.

Although Yorkshire Terriers had a separate stud book entry by 1862, they were still classed under the Scotch Terrier for show purposes. When The Kennel Club was founded in 1873, its stud book was compiled, so pedigrees of principal winners to that date were available. Breeds were then divided into Sporting and Non-sporting, our Yorkshire being Non-sporting, but the breeds were less clearly defined – many would have been entered in the stud book as various toy terriers. It was not until 1886 that the Kennel Club actually recognised them. Consequently, the Scots said goodbye to their Scotch Terrier, and our glamorous, long-haired Toy finally became known only as the Yorkshire Terrier. Finally our little dog had his own identity and home where, over the years to come, he would keep the now extinct Paisley/Clydesdale blood still flowing through his veins.

*Huddersfield Ben (left)
with Mrs Gifford's 'Kate'.*

This new breed soon attracted many admirers who took up the fancy: Peter Eden of Salford, Lancashire, Mr Inman and Mr Burgess of Brighouse, Yorkshire, and Mr J. Spink, who owned Bounce, grandsire to Huddersfield Ben, and also Sandy, sire of Lady, Huddersfield Ben's dam.

HUDDERSFIELD BEN
We now come to the year 1865, when a dog was born who was not only going to put his stamp on the breed, but would forever be known as 'The Father of the Breed': Huddersfield Ben, Kennel Stud Book No. 3612. His debut in the ring was at Manchester, where he won second prize as a 'Scotch Terrier'. Bred by Mr Eastwood of Huddersfield, Yorkshire, and shown at this show as owned by Mr J. Foster, thereafter he was in the ownership of Mrs Jonas

PEDIGREE OF HUDDERSFIELD BEN

Boscovitchs Dog			
	Ramsdens Bounce	Ramsdens Bob	Haigh's Teddy
			Old Dolly
		Old Dolly	Albert
			N/K
	Lady (Eastwoods)	Old Ben	Eastwoods Ramsdens Bounce
			Young Dolly
		Young Dolly	Old Sandy
			Old Dolly

Foster, of Bradford, Yorkshire. Ben's pedigree is interesting as his dam is also his sire's dam. Mr Foster's veterinary surgeon sums up the dog in *Ladies' Dogs as Companions*, 1876:

Now, of all the Yorkshire Terriers ever I saw, I think Huddersfield Ben was the Best. Many of my readers doubtless remember this most beautiful prince of dogs, although it is now some few years since he was run over on the street and killed, he being then only in his prime. But he did not die before he had made his mark. Dog shows were not then quite so numerous as they are now, but nevertheless Ben managed to win seventy-four prizes ere his grand career was shortened on that unlucky 23rd September 1871.

Pedigrees, few ladies I believe care to remember, so I shall not give Ben's in full, but be content with stating that he was bred by Mr W. Eastwood, Huddersfield, and had the blood of Old Bounce in his veins, and his mother, Lady, was a daughter of Old Ben, a granddaughter of Old Sandy, and a great-granddaughter of Mr W.J. Haigh's Teddy, and a great-

great-granddaughter of Mr J. Swift's Old Crab. I am the very worst genealogist in the world, so I cannot go back any further for fear of running on shore somewhere. Perhaps, though, Old Crab came over with the Conqueror – from Scotland you know.

Assuming this information is correct, we can trace Ben's ancestors back even further through an article by Mr E. Bootman of Halifax, Yorkshire, which appeared in *The English Stockkeeper* in about 1887.

Mrs M.A. Foster's 'Prince'.
Sire: 'Peter' (by 'Huddersfield Ben').
Dam: 'Lady' (by 'Bruce').

'Yorkshire Terrier with a Ball'.
Initialed 'CD' and dated 1877.
Photo: Iona Antiques.

Swift's Old Crab, a cross-bred Scotch Terrier, Kershaw's Kitty, a Skye, and an Old English Terrier bitch kept by J. Whittam, then residing in Hatter's Fold, Halifax, were the progenitors of the present race of Yorkshire Terriers. These dogs were in the zenith of their fame 40 years ago. The owner of Old Crab was a native of Halifax, and a joiner by trade. He worked at Oldham for some time as a joineryman and then removed to Manchester, where he kept a public house. Whether he got Crab at Oldham or Manchester I have not been able to ascertain. He had him when in Manchester, and from there sent him several times to Halifax on a visit to Kitty. The last would be about 1850.

Crab was a dog of about eight or nine pounds weight, with a good Terrier head and eye, but with a long body, resembling the Scotch Terrier. The legs and muzzle only were tanned, and the hair on the body would be about three or four inches in length. He has stood for years in a case in a room at the Westgate Hotel, a public house which his owner kept when he returned to his native town, where, I believe, the dog may be seen today.

Kitty was a bitch different in type from Crab. She was a drop-eared Skye, with plenty of coat of a blue shade, but destitute of tan on any part of the body. Like Crab, she had no pedigree. She was originally stolen from Manchester and sent to a man named Jackson, a saddler in Huddersfield, who, when it became known that a five pound reward was offered in Manchester for her recovery, sent her to a person named Harrison, then a waiter at the White Swan Hotel, Halifax, to escape detection, and from Harrison she passed into the hand of Mr J. Kershaw of Bishop Blaise, a public house which once stood on the Old North Bridge, Halifax. Prior to 1851 Kitty had six litters, all of which were by Crab. In these six litters she had 36 puppies, 28 of which were dogs, and served to stock the district with rising sires. After 1851, when she passed into the possession of Mr F. Jagger, she had 44 puppies, making a total of 80.

Mr Whittam's bitch, whose name I cannot get to know, was an Old English Terrier, with tanned head, ears and legs, and a sort of grizzle back. She was built on the lines of speed. Like the others, she had no pedigree. She was sent to the late Bernard Hartley of Allen Gate, Halifax, by a friend residing in Scotland. When Mr Hartley had got tired of her, he gave her to his coachman, Mason, who in turn gave her to his friend Whittam, and Whittam used her years for breeding purposes.

Although this bitch came from Scotland, it is believed the parents were from this district.

OLD SANDY

We are able to look even further into Ben's ancestry, thanks to old records. From *Dogs: Their Points, Whims, Instincts and Peculiarities*, a book edited and published in 1872, we find mention of Crab and Kitty's grandson; he appears in Ben's pedigree as a great-grandparent, a great-great-grandparent and a great-great-great-grandparent. He was Old Sandy, registered at the Kennel Club as a Yorkshire Terrier, although Ben beat him into the registry. According to Mr Webb, Old Sandy "was seven pounds, a very rich tan, golden head, deep blue and a very straight, rather strong, hair, but very bright." Unfortunately, he was stolen on his way home from Brighton in 1866, after winning first prize at a dog show.

On the subject of breeding the 'Scotch Terrier', Old Sandy's owner, Mr Spink, said:

The head rather long, with hair falling down considerably below the jaw, golden colour at the sides and on ears, also on the muzzle and mustachios; hair on the back long and perfectly straight, good rich blue and very bright; legs and feet well tanned and not too much feathered; tail perfectly straight and well carried; shape firm and compact, not too long on the legs, broad chest and tanned; there must be no white on any part of the body, not even the

'Heady study of a Yorkshire Terrier'. Signed M. Cocker, inscribed: 'Prize Yorkshire Terrier, Mrs Rogers, Plymouth'. c. 1890.

'A study of a Terrier'. Signed and dated 'Ada L. Pinney, 1910'. Photo: Iona Antiques.

slightest suspicion of curl or wave on the coat, and the hair fine and bright in quality. The blue and tan should contrast so well as to please the eye, rich and decided in colour, and not a sickly silver colour all over.

I think we can assume that the forming of the Yorkshire Terrier was certainly not a haphazard affair – there were breeders who knew exactly what they wanted in their 'Toy Terrier' and bred for it. Through controlled in-breeding, they finally produced our delightful friend, the Yorkshire Terrier.

Although he had only a short life, Huddersfield Ben's impact as a sire was great. He set the pattern for all future Yorkshire Terriers. Mrs Foster took the affix Bradford and exhibited progeny sired by Ben, namely Little Kate, Bruce, Emperor, Sandy, Spring and Tyler. Then there was Bradford Marie, at 0.8kg (1lb 14oz), and the smallest recorded Yorkie of that time – Bradford Queen of the Toys – weighing in at 0.7kg (1lb 8oz).

Ben was responsible for the increased popularity of the breed. He was a dominant sire, producing puppies of true colour and type. For his time, he was the optimum of the breed, so demand for him as stud dog was considerable. He sired many good winners for other kennels: Little Kate, Bismark, Mr J. Hill's Sandy, Benson, Bruce, Doctor Spark (also exhibited by Mr J. Stell as Charley) and Emperor, and many other well-known dogs of the

Early 20th century postcard depicting a lady with a Yorkshire Terrier.

time. His son, Mozart, out of Frisk, born in 1869 and owned by Miss Alderson, won 105 prizes in all, including Birmingham and Nottingham Shows in 1873. He was awarded a first prize at Westmorland in the year 1870. Up until then, Yorkies were still being shown in other classes (such as in the broken-haired Scotch Terriers class) so we can look on Frisk as being the first dog to win consistently in Yorkshire Terrier classes.

THE FIRST BREED CLUB
As the Yorkshire Terrier became

established as a breed, various breed clubs were formed to promote the interests of the breed and to provide information to interested parties. The first of these to be formed was the Yorkshire Terrier Club, founded in 1898, twelve years after the breed's official recognition by the Kennel Club.

The club's mission statement declared its objective to be "to promote the interests of the breed". During the period 1920-1930 registrations for Yorkshire Terriers numbered 150-200 a year. However, by the early 1930s, the breed's popularity had increased by 50 per cent. The club was adhering to its mission statement objective, and the breed was thriving as a result.

During the Second World War, the club records were kept in a bank for safety, and the club did not become active again until 1946. By 1950 registrations had increased to 1,217.

As Britain recovered from the doldrums of the 50s, a boom-time was emerging in the 60s. There was generally plenty of jobs, money and leisure time. This was reflected in how many more people took up the fancy of the Yorkshire Terrier. By 1967, registrations had risen to 7,389. This increased to 13,780 in 1973 – almost a 100 per cent increase in

six years! Registrations have dropped steadily since then: 12,755 in 1982, 10,877 in 1996 and 8,818 in 1998. However, in relative terms, the Yorkie is still as popular as ever – usually reaching the top 10 in the KC – and AKC – annual registration figures.

ARRIVING IN AMERICA
The Yorkshire Terrier found himself in America by 1870, four years before the American Kennel Club was founded. The first Yorkie to have an AKC-registered number was Butch (born 1882), an imported dog who was bred by A. Webster in England and owned by Charles Andrews from Bloomington, Illinois. He also owned a second AKC-registered Yorkshire Terrier, Daisy, who was born in 1884. The breeder is unknown. (For more on the breed in America, see Chapter 12).

The Yorkie's popularity is now worldwide, with many new clubs coming into existence to join the well-established ones. Australia, South Africa, New Zealand and Europe all boast of their speciality clubs, and now the Yorkshire Terrier is also finding new horizons in Russia. From his humble beginnings, he is certainly now a very well-travelled dog.

3 THE YORKSHIRE TERRIER PUPPY

Your choice of a Yorkshire Terrier will not disappoint you. Once you have owned one, you will always want to own one. A Yorkie pup is one of the most delightful of pups – a black-and-tan bundle of fluff, with a cheeky face and piercing black eyes full of mischief.

SELF-ASSESSMENT

Buying a puppy should be a happy and very rewarding experience, gaining for you a loyal companion for many years to come. However, you must take your decision to buy a new pup very seriously. Consider your present circumstances and plans for the future. Are they compatible with dog ownership? If not, wait for a more suitable time when you are better prepared for the commitment.

Your Yorkie may live with you almost as long as a child, and will be around the home a lot more. A child goes to school, meets friends etc., but a dog will be around all the time.

If you have children in the house, are they old enough, or responsible enough, to have a puppy in the house? It is easy for a young child to treat such a small dog as a toy. Clumsy fingers can cause considerable pain to him, and dropping him from relatively minor heights can result in broken bones or death. If you have young children and are determined the Yorkie is the breed for you, opt for a larger, more robust type.

Remember also that a vibrant puppy grows sluggish with old age and may be inflicted with illness and disease in the future. His age will demand greater care and attention. Beyond his physical needs are certain psychological ones. A dog needs more than food, drink, and exercise; he also needs a certain amount of play and love. He needs to feel part of the family.

Before buying, you should also consider what other pets you have. If you are introducing a puppy into the domain of a very elderly cat, he will not take kindly to the new intruder, and it may be best to wait until he is no longer around. And a large dog can cause injury to a small pup even with a simple knock.

Do you have the time and patience needed for the training and grooming commitments a new pup brings? A Yorkie needs at least 15 minutes every day, to avoid knotting and matting, and training is an on-going process continuing into the dog's adulthood.

COST OF CARE
The next consideration should be whether you can afford a dog. You may

Taking on a Yorkshire Terrier is a big commitment, so think carefully before making your final decision.

Photo: Amanda Bulbeck.

be able to make the initial outlay for the pup, but can you meet the ongoing expenses? Because of his size, a Yorkie is relatively cheap to feed, but other costs soon mount up: veterinary treatment, regular worming and flea treatments, pet insurance premiums, bedding, collar and lead, grooming equipment, toys, training costs, professional grooming, and kennel fees etc.

FINDING A GOOD BREEDER

Contact your nearest breed club for a list of people who have pups available (your national Kennel Club should be able to provide contact details of local clubs). Many discerning buyers are prepared to wait up to six months for their pride and joy. So do be selective and patient; this bundle of fluff is going to be with you for many years, so a little wait is worthwhile in the end.

Where you purchase your pup is your decision, but remember the saying 'buyer beware!'. Take care to buy your puppy from a reputable breeder, and certainly not from a puppy farm (mill) or from someone who is just breeding for profit and has no concern for improving the breed and for producing healthy pups. Possibly the best two options for buying a pup are the breed specialist and the person who has decided to have a litter from a pet bitch, hopefully using a quality stud dog.

MEETING THE BREEDER

No breeder will want to bring a stranger in to see or handle the pups while their eyes are still shut, and, for the sake of not upsetting the dam, probably not until the pups are weaned. Be guided by the breeder and remember that very young pups bear very little resemblance to the mature adult.

Always make an appointment in advance to see a litter, and if you are just looking, do not expect to handle the pups – there is a risk of you passing on infection if you have been to other kennels.

A responsible breeder will help you to choose the puppy that will suit your lifestyle. Photo: Steve Nash.

Always remember that, wherever you purchase your pup, there are no guarantees that you are buying from a good breeder. You should always be observant when viewing a litter: the premises should be clean and the puppies should appear healthy and lively.

In your search for the ideal breeder you should be looking for someone who has experience of the breed, who owns the dam, someone who rears in the home, offers after-sales advice and is willing to take the puppies back if there are any problems. If you have doubts about the breeder, contact some others until you are confident you have found the best.

Your pup should have been reared with much care and devotion. When you go to buy your bundle of joy, be completely honest about your requirements and, ultimately, be sure you want the pup. I once had customers who came for a pup and thought they were buying an Airedale Terrier! To them, a terrier was a terrier. They were soon put in the right direction, but they were quite prepared to take my pup on the chance that it would grow and grow. If you have the slightest doubt about buying a puppy, do not be embarrassed to back out; it is far more desirable than committing half-heartedly and having to find the poor soul another home a few months later.

It is not easy to resist a cute bundle of fluff with those appealing eyes, but if you are unhappy with the pup, mum, environment or breeder in any way, do not consider buying him – you will only be disappointed with your new pet and you may incur expensive vet bills.

MEETING THE PUPS

Badly reared pups will show many obvious signs: dirty ears may indicate mites; listlessness and dull eyes may be a sign of worms; nasal discharge may mean respiratory infection; bald patches may suggest mange or ringworm; excessive scratching can mean fleas; and diarrhoea may indicate worms or intestinal infection. There should be no enlargement of the leg joints or any other deformities in the feet or legs, as rickets (caused by a bad diet) could be present.

Healthy pups will be well-fed and well-groomed with bright, clear eyes. They should be active and greet you with enthusiasm. There is no mistaking

A well-reared litter will be clean, healthy and alert. *Photo: Steve Nash.*

The ears may be erect or semi-erect.
Photo: Steve Nash.

a bunch of healthy Yorkie pups: they are fearless balls of fluff, tearing around making little yips and playing.

The young pups' ears may be erect or semi-erect. A pup often drops one or both ears when teething. Many do not have erect ears until they are five or six months old.

You should meet the dam and assess her character: is she friendly, nervous or aggressive? Remember the pups may grow up to be like their dam; would you be happy about this? Perhaps you can also meet Grandma or Grandpa. All breeders worth their salt are proud of their stock and only too pleased to show off their dogs. If the breeder is not prepared for you to meet the dam, be very wary, as the pups could have been bought in from a puppy farm.

As well as assessing the breeder and puppies, remember that you will have to convince a reputable breeder that you are able to offer a suitable home. Expect to undergo a thorough interrogation!

CHOOSING YOUR PUPPY

MALE OR FEMALE?
Whether you have a boy or a girl will be a personal decision, as both sexes are delightful. Many say the bitch is more loyal, but I have never found this; I find the dogs much more devoted and easier to train. However, all my girls are great fun and absolute extroverts, so the sex is immaterial to me. A male has the advantage of not coming into season every six or eight months.

TAIL
In the UK and the US, Yorkies are customarily docked. Some people prefer a Yorkie with a tail. Really, it's a matter of individual choice. If you would like one with a tail, tell your breeder this before the litter is born, as docking is performed by a vet when pups are three to four days old. You may have to pay a deposit for the privilege, as breeders may be concerned that you will drop out and they will be left with a pup that may be difficult to sell. In the US it is even more rare to see a Yorkie with a tail.

Many specialised breeders feel very strongly about Yorkies with tails and believe that a tail can unbalance the overall picture and make the dog look too long. Many breeders will not comply with your wishes, since, at four days, it is impossible for a breeder to select the right puppy for you – the undocked dog may turn out to be the

Male or female? Some say a bitch (left) is more loyal, but most males are equally devoted. Photo: Steve Nash.

best in the litter, in which case, the whole purpose of breeding the litter would have been lost.

If you buy a pup with a tail, do make sure its dewclaws have been removed, as these can cause trouble as the pup grows, getting caught up in clothing and combs.

SIZE

Size is the one factor over which breeders have little control. Breeders' attempts to produce smaller dogs for the show ring resulted in tiny bitches too small for breeding. The larger bitches were mated to smaller dogs, and so the offspring from these matings varied considerably in size.

A large bitch can produce a small dog, and vice versa. Although some dogs only produce small, you usually find you have something else to contend with, like colour. You must decide what you want. Country dwellers are usually happy with a large Yorkie of up to 4.5kg (10lb), while city dwellers prefer a smaller dog, weighing 1.8–2.7kg (4–6lb); your living style will decide this. In any case, the pup is never going to grow into a large dog.

THE SHOW PROSPECT

If you are considering a show puppy, visit a dog show. This will give you an opportunity to introduce yourself to specialist breeders who are always willing to help. You will also be able to view the various strains of dogs shown. It will also be worth joining your nearest breed club and attending one of their shows.

Be honest with your breeder about your requirements, and let them know if you would like a dog to show. No one has bought a great show dog by buying a pet, so do not think that the cheaper pet puppy will grow into an exquisite show dog. Be prepared to wait until a suitable pup becomes available.

Show dogs do not grow on trees. A fine, mature adult takes not months but years to mature. Some do mature earlier, but they are the exception rather than the rule, and these dogs often have other refinements that surpass their contemporaries. Many breeders have kept a puppy for up to a year, only to find their high-flyer turns out to be a turkey.

The chances of purchasing a show dog at eight weeks are very slim. Indeed, many breeders will not part with a pup wanted for showing until he is at least four months of age. A puppy of six months is more of a sure bet as you will have more of an indication of what he will look like as an adult. Even then, his colour at this age cannot guarantee he will finish as a fine specimen. However, at six months, he should be showing promise with an ample wealth of coat. Blue and black colours should be evident, and especially the tan clearing into golden tan. The texture should feel like silk.

At 12-18 months, a junior dog will be exhibiting all the attributes and showing his future promise. Practically in full coat, his coat colour should nearly now be established as to its quality and depth of colour, only needing his maturity for it to finish to a rich golden tan and steel blue, and, of course, length. A dog like this is nearly impossible to buy since if

The show prospect: The breeder can help you to choose a puppy with show potential, but there can be no guarantee of success.

Ch. Verolian Puccini at eight weeks.

Ch. Verolian Puccini at 17 months. Note his head is not a clear tan yet, and the blue is not broken. This can take up to three years.

he is that good, he will be kept by his breeder. Only if the breeder is overstocked with equally good dogs will he consider him for sale – ensuring the dog's quality is reflected in the price.

When looking for a pup with show potential (say between the ages of 12 and 16 weeks), you should look for a level topline, his legs should be quite straight, and he should look quite balanced (i.e. the length of back should be in proportion to the dog's height).

The head should be genteel and kind in expression. The ears should be neat and well-placed on top of his head. The nose should be dark, and the eyes should also be dark and mischievous-looking.

His mouth should have a scissor-bite (where the upper teeth closely overlap the lower ones). If, at this age, his mouth is not quite correct, a chance can be taken that the mouth will rectify itself, but not if it is badly overshot or undershot.

The pup's coat should be showing assurance of its future colour and fine texture. It should be abundant, fine and silky to the touch. Make sure that no light blue is breaking at the roots, and check the legs for the promise of golden tan in the future. Check behind the ears – the colour here should be bright and tan, and is generally a good guide to his final tan colouring.

He should display a healthy disposition, being plump and rounded. The Yorkie pup should also be pleased to see you. Never consider a show prospect who appears nervous, backs away from you, or who is aggressive in any way.

Ch. Beezneez Tetley Bitter:
An ideal head for a six-month-old pup.

Ch. Clantalon Contention as
a 10-month-old puppy.

Ch. Verolian Out Of
The Blue – the
finished article.

Remember that a pup must be registered with your national Kennel Club if you wish to show him. A male must also have two testicles fully descended in the scrotum if you intend to exhibit.

PREPARING FOR YOUR PUP

Make sure you make the necessary changes to your garden before the puppy comes home. It should be fully escape-proof. A small puppy can get through a very tiny hole. Yorkies are so inquisitive – they love rummaging in hedges, hunting for imaginary monsters. If you have a hedge which your pup can get through, some chicken wire should be erected around the perimeter – around three feet in height should be sufficient. If you have a wooden fence, make sure it is solid, with no holes that can be escaped through. Put a sign on the gate ('Please shut the gate, dog loose'), or put a spring on the gate so it closes automatically.

Before you collect your puppy, make sure you have all the necessary equipment. I've always found this can be as exciting as purchasing the actual pup. Most people collecting their pup have bought everything from nylon bones, coats, enough toys to fill a box, and enough food to see the pup through a famine, not to mention the fancy collars and leads.

The puppy's requirements are few. Nevertheless, he will need a few basic items to begin with.

BED
Your dog's bed is very important. As a pup, he will spend many hours sleeping, so make sure it is comfortable and easy to clean. Initially, a cardboard box cut down at the front and lined with newspaper and a blanket (or fleece bedding) is quite suitable.

Hard plastic beds are clean and hygienic and can have very comfortable linings that can be changed and washed. Bean beds are comfortable and washable, too.

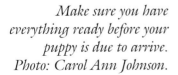

Make sure you have everything ready before your puppy is due to arrive. Photo: Carol Ann Johnson.

COLLAR AND LEAD

There is an abundant choice of collars and leads – from leather and cloth through to nylon and jewel-encrusted ones. The problem with having a Yorkie, is trying to find a collar which is small enough to fit. I usually buy the smallest soft puppy collar I can find, even if this entails punching in a couple of extra holes. I never let the dogs wear their collars in the house because it can ruin their precious coats.

Put the new collar on the puppy for a few hours a day and he will soon become used to his 'necklace'. This will make lead-training far easier.

IDENTIFICATION

Any dog out in a public place should have an identity disc (tag) attached to his collar, giving the dog's name and a contact telephone number. Many pet shops have an immediate engraving service.

Microchipping and tattooing are other forms of identification. All puppies born in Germany must be tattooed before leaving their house of birth. The tattoo takes the form of a number which is put inside the ear. The number is then recorded on their registration papers so no mistake can be made regarding the dog's identity.

In countries where tattooing is optional, some Yorkie enthusiasts choose other means of identification, believing that the tattoo is unsightly – especially so in a prick-eared dog.

Microchipping can be done through your vet, who will inject a tiny chip into your dog's body – usually between the shoulder blades. The chip has its own unique number which can be identified by passing an electronic scanner over the dog's body. The number can then be checked against a register to find the owner's contact details.

BOWLS

Some Yorkies can react to stainless steel bowls – either being distracted by the reflection, or trying to play with it. If your Yorkie reacts to the reflection and you get fed up with wet floors, change to a china or plastic bowl.

TOYS

All Yorkies love toys and yours will be no exception. There is a countless assortment on the market – from rubber to rope, from hide chews to furry toys.

Like all dogs with a terrier background, the squeaky toy is a firm favourite and will give hours of enjoyment, but do check the squeak regularly as it can become dislodged and end up being swallowed. As soon as the toy becomes damaged, replace it.

COLLECTING YOUR PUP

The time has come to collect your pup from your breeder. The pup should be round and plump, and bright-eyed. His coat should be glossy and his general appearance should reflect his excellent condition. He should have been wormed and be ready for you to take home from eight to ten weeks. Some mothers adore their pups and the breeder will not let them go until they are 10-12 weeks of age, but this is the exception rather than the rule.

When you collect your precious pup, you will be given his pedigree, registration and a diet sheet. This diet should be strictly adhered to, since you don't want your new addition to have an upset tum as soon as you bring it home.

JOURNEY HOME
You must make sure the journey home with your new puppy is not too traumatic. It will be the first time he has been alone with you, and you do not want him to associate you with a very unpleasant experience.

He will be nervous being away from his familiar surroundings, but do your best to limit his stress.

If you are collecting your pup by public transport, make sure you take along a suitable carrying box. There are some very reasonable plastic ones on the market that will continue to come in useful when you need to take your Yorkie to the vet. His box, lined with a towel or blanket from his previous home (and so carrying a familiar scent), should make him feel snug and secure.

A car journey will not be so traumatic for him as he will not be under the scrutiny of members of the public, but instead in the arms of his new family. It is wise to ask a friend to drive, so you can hold the pup in your arms or on a blanket on your lap and reassure him during the journey.

It is a good idea to have a roll of kitchen towel on hand in case the pup salivates or is sick. Not many pups are sick on their first journey, especially if the breeder has ensured the pup's stomach is empty. Most breeders will agree a time for you to collect the puppy for this very reason; he would have had his last meal a couple of hours prior to your arrival.

No puppy under 12 weeks should endure a journey of four hours or more as it can be dehydrating and exhausting for him, and can result in him needing veterinary treatment. Even if the distance between the breeder and your home is very short, make sure you take a bowl and some fresh water to give the puppy if you get stuck in some unexpected traffic, or break down.

THE FIRST NIGHT

On arriving home, your pup will be bewildered and a little lost, having just left his mother and litter-mates. Put him in the kitchen and let him sniff around. Show the pup his bed; he won't like that, as his intention is to find where you sleep and make that his bed! Offer a drink; warm caffeinated tea with milk is always acceptable to a Yorkie. Talk to him, calling him by name and, within a very short time, your Yorkie will be rushing around as though he was born there. Be patient, especially as regards toilet training.

Your puppy's first night will be the deciding factor on where he will sleep in the future. Once the pup has experienced the warmth of your bed, you won't be able to go back and expect him to sleep alone in the kitchen a couple of days later. If you 'give in' to the heart-rending, sorrowful howls on the first night, be prepared to share your bed for the next fifteen years!

Yorkies are great heat-lovers, so make

Do not be surprised if your puppy feels a little bewildered when he first gets home.

sure the room your pup is sleeping in is a comfortable temperature – not too hot and certainly not too cold. Make sure his bed is not in a draught.

When you put your pup to bed, tell him "Good night". All my dogs now know the meaning of these words and will settle for the night. If the howling and crying begins, firmly tell the pup – through the door – to be quiet. If this does not work, put a hot-water bottle in his bed and a ticking clock in the room – these items emulate the warmth and heartbeat of the pup's littermates and dam.

Do bear in mind that, in one day, he has lost the company of his brothers and sisters, his adoring mother and his first human owner, the breeder. This must be very perplexing for such a young animal, so be patient. It should only take a few days for the pup to settle and be content sleeping alone.

Yorkies are very determined creatures, so do not be surprised if, despite your best efforts, they end up calling all the shots. When I first got my Mitzi, I was determined that she would sleep in the kitchen, since another Yorkie, Cindy, already shared my bed. The first night was hell, as Mitzi howled all night. The second night, she was put to bed with a hot-water bottle, a ticking clock and a cuddly toy. She was fine up to midnight and then howled until dawn. Not to be beaten by a tiny ball of fur, on the third evening I took her for a long walk in the garden before settling her to bed, but it was just a repeat of the second night! By the fourth night, I compromised and moved her bedding into my bedroom, but she spent the entire night trying to leap on to the bed. She only succeeded in nearly knocking herself out, and keeping me and Cindy awake with the continual thud on the side of the bed. Inevitably, she got her own way on the fifth night, and spent the rest of her nights with me! She never failed to get what she wanted throughout her life.

EARLY DAYS

For the first couple of days, keep the pup quiet, giving him time to settle into his new home. Do not let the entire neighbourhood come around to see him. You will be dying to show off this wonderful ball of fluff, but do think of your puppy – it can be quite overwhelming for him while he is still trying to get used to his new surroundings. There is plenty of time to socialise him once he is a little more settled (see Chapter Four).

HOUSE-TRAINING

It would be perfect if the young puppy could be fully house-trained at a few weeks of age. Unfortunately, this chore is usually left to the new owner. If your puppy is 12 weeks or older, expect him to be reasonably house-trained. He may temporarily forget his training in his new surroundings, but as soon as you

get him into a regular routine, becoming accustomed to the new smells, he will remember what he has been taught.

If you live in an apartment, or have a winter pup and the weather is too inclement to go out, you will have to paper-train the pup. Spread out newspaper in the area where you want the pup to relieve himself – perhaps by the backdoor. Whatever spot you choose, keep this area separate from the pup's sleeping area, as they do not like 'fouling' their 'nest'.

Place the pup on the paper regularly throughout the day, including: when he

Intelligent and quick to learn, the Yorkie puppy will soon get the idea of house-training.

wakes in the morning; before and after every meal; before and after exercise; and at night before going to bed. If you see your pup squatting, or circling and sniffing the ground, grab him at once and place him on the paper.

Each time he uses the paper, make much of him and give a treat as a reward. He will soon realise that, by using the paper, he is pleasing you.

Occasionally, the pup will have an accident. On no account, shout at him, hit him, or rub his nose in the mess. You will simply upset him unnecessarily and achieve nothing. Always wash the fouled area with disinfectant that will remove the smell and so prevent him from returning to the area again.

A summer pup is easier to house-train since you can leave the backdoor open for the pup to go out whenever the need arises. Instead of getting your Yorkie used to paper, get him used to going outside on a chosen spot in the garden. As with paper-training, he should be taken out regularly and should be praised for performing. When he is eliminating, say a word such as 'busy' and he will come to associate the word with the action.

If the weather was particularly bad when you first got your Yorkie, you may have partially trained him on paper. To get him to perform outdoors, take some newspaper outside with the pup. Put it on the ground and encourage him to squat on it. Being familiar with the paper, he should perform quickly. As this progresses, reduce the size of the paper gradually until you do not need to use newspaper any more.

Take your pup out regularly so he comes to associate his toilet with going out. Whenever he performs, give lots of praise and let him have a quick play before going indoors. As time passes and he grows into an adult, you can gradually lengthen the times between going out.

CARING FOR YOUR PUPPY

INOCULATIONS
Your vet will inoculate your pup against distemper, leptospirosis, parvovirus, hepatitis and para influenza. A rabies shot may also need to be given if you are in a country where this disease is a problem (mandatory in the U.S.). Do not delay in contacting your vet for the injections to be given – visitors can bring in germs and I'm sure you will want to take the puppy out for little walks and to lead-train him. Until the vaccinations are complete, do not put your pup at risk by letting him socialise with other dogs, or by taking him out where other dogs may have been. If you have other dogs at home, and they are up to date with their vaccinations, your new puppy is not at any risk from mixing with them.

WORMING
Your pup should have been wormed at his place of birth, and you should tell your vet the date of the last worming

and the product used, so that he or she can tell you when the pup will need worming again.

EXERCISE

Control your puppy's exercise in the early months. Jumping from a settee can cause damage to the pup's delicate limbs, as can racing round the garden like a lunatic. Let your puppy play – but do control it. I am sure more damage is done to a Yorkie's limbs by over-exuberant play than any other factor, so remember that their joints and bones are very soft and delicate. For the first year they can easily damage their little limbs.

Never let a puppy up and down the stairs until he is about a year old. To restrict access to the stairs, use a stair-gate, or make sure all doors are closed. Watch the pup closely on his first encounter and be ready to grab him in case he falls. It could be that the dog always remains too small to be able to manage the stairs, in which case you will always have to carry him up and down them.

When placing a pup down on the floor, always put him down gently and never allow him to leap out of anyone's arms on to the floor. It could cause concussion or broken bones, or could even be fatal.

Whether your dog is a pet or show dog, he will need exercise to keep fit. The show dog needs exercise throughout the day, to keep mentally fit and to build up muscle.

FEEDING

When you purchase your Yorkie pup, the breeder will give you a diet sheet. For the first few weeks, do try to adhere to this; to change the diet immediately would only result in the puppy having an upset tummy. If, after a couple of weeks, you wish to change his food, do it gradually by introducing the new food in small amounts to his usual food, and then increasing the level until the changeover is complete.

Without the competition of brothers and sisters, eating is not so exciting for your puppy. From this early age, he will

Exercise should be limited for the first couple of months.

To begin with, your puppy will miss the rivalry of his littermates at mealtimes.
Photo: Carol Ann Johnson.

try to manipulate you into feeding only the best chicken or beef – and whatever you are eating! Remember that no dog will deliberately starve himself, but a Yorkie can make you become very concerned.

A typical diet sheet is as follows:

BREAKFAST (7.30-8am) 2-4 oz (57-114 grammes) of complete puppy food.
LUNCH (1pm) Repeat of breakfast.
DINNER (5-6pm) 2-4 oz (57-114 grammes) of minced (chopped) beef or other red meat, tripe, or finely chopped chicken.

For a young puppy, routine is very important. Stick to meal times as near as possible, since his digestive system becomes accustomed to the set times of receiving food.

Your Yorkie pup can be kept on this routine diet for up to five months. If he leaves his 1pm feed, cut it out altogether. You can increase the quantities of his other feeds as he grows or seems hungrier.

By 12 months, his stomach will be large enough for him to eat a day's food at one or two meals. I personally feed two meals a day to all my adults: breakfast (consisting of a complete food) and a meat dinner in the evening.

You will most likely have to adjust the amount of food and meal-times to suit your particular Yorkie and his needs.

GROOMING SESSIONS
Mats are not only unsightly but can be very painful. If your Yorkie scratches, his hind nails can become lodged in them. Removing mats can also be uncomfortable, so regular grooming is essential. Start your pup's grooming from when you first bring him home. You will need a good-quality brush – preferably a bristle one – and a wide-toothed comb.

Place the pup on your lap, holding him securely, and brush his coat and gently comb it. Pay particular attention to his elbows, thighs and belly. Be gentle about his head, taking care not to poke him in the eye; always comb from the eye down the nose. Have a grooming session at the same time each day; soon the puppy will look forward to it and be no stranger to brushes and combs. This is especially important if you want to have him clipped later on at the grooming parlour.

The tan hair around your pup's

bottom should be kept cut short to prevent fouling. Hopefully, the breeder will have done this already and shown you exactly where to trim; if not, it is the tan hair under the tail.

Since Yorkies do not shed, their hair will grow and grow. The accumulation of natural oil in their coats makes them greasy, so regular bathing is needed. Each dog differs. I find some need a bath weekly and others only monthly; some are naturally clean and others not so clean.

Often I have found that a four- or five-month-old puppy's coat can appear dry. In such a case, I now add half a teaspoon of sunflower oil to his food. This is marvellous for dry skin, and adding that little bit of oil is always an asset to a Yorkie's coat.

As your Yorkie matures, his coat will thicken. This can often be a problem in today's busy world. If you cannot spare the time to look after the coat properly, take your pet Yorkie to a grooming parlour and have him clipped and bathed rather than have a matted, smelly dog. Your dog will then not only look attractive, but be easier to keep clean.

BATHING AND DRYING
It is best to wash your Yorkie in the bath with a spray. Wet the pup all over with warm water, wetting the head last. Apply a good proprietary dog shampoo, making sure to avoid his eyes. Lather up well and rinse off. Add conditioner

A six-month-old pup oiled up and starting her crackers.

A pet trim looks very attractive, and is obviously far easier to maintain.

and rinse, making sure no residue is left. Squeeze as much excess water as possible out of the coat and towel it dry, finishing off with a hair-dryer to make sure it is quite dry. Brush and comb through.

From four to six months of age, a show dog will then have a fine coating of oil, preferably almond, applied to the coat with a bristle brush, and the coat is parted down the back. The 'finished product' is very attractive.

EARS

Check your Yorkie's ears weekly for ear mites, especially if there are cats around who may be able to pass on the mites. If your pup has ear mites, there will be a dark brown discharge and a pungent smell from his ears. If ear-mites are present, your pup needs to see a vet, and he is likely to be prescribed proprietary ear cleaner.

NAILS

Your puppy's nails will need to be cut occasionally. How often depends on how fast he wears them down. Any nails left to grow too long can cause problems by getting caught up or being pulled out, or curling back and pressing into the pads. The pup (or adult) will be unable to grip smooth surfaces and the nails will snag on rugs.

To cut his nails, invest in a pair of guillotine nail clippers. As the Yorkie's nails are black, it is better to leave too much as opposed to too little, as you will not be able to see the quick of the nail. Snip off the end of the nail – the narrow bit that starts to form the hook. If you do cut the quick by accident, apply a little potassium permanganate to stop the bleeding.

Yorkies can give out the most horrendous wails when having their nails cut. I have never cut the quicks of my dogs' nails and yet they seem sure they are about to lose a leg, even with the kindest reassurance. Getting them used to the routine procedure when they are very small should minimise their distress when adult.

If you are at all hesitant about cutting the nails, have a vet or professional groomer clip them, and watch and learn.

TEETH

In my experience, a Yorkshire Terrier puppy's teeth are usually through at between eight and ten weeks of age, as opposed to larger breeds whose teeth may be through at three to four weeks. When all the milk teeth are through, you will soon know it, as they are like little pins. Your puppy should be given chews or chew-toys at this time to give him an outlet for his need to gnaw. Some puppies can become uncomfortable while teething, so remember that his gums are sore, and be particularly sympathetic.

Even at this early stage, it is worth getting your pup used to having his teeth brushed. Either use a finger brush or a toothbrush. Special meat-flavoured toothpastes are available to make the whole experience far more enjoyable for your Yorkie.

The milk teeth will start to drop out at about five to six months. The pup's gums may be sore and spots of blood may appear on things he chews. Do not worry, this is normal. If he has been fed well on a balanced diet, his teeth should grow in straight and strong. Sometimes, however, the permanent teeth appear before the milk teeth have fallen out. This can result in the mouth becoming crooked.

If your Yorkie pup has problems shedding his first canines, your vet will be required to remove the offending milk teeth. This is a small operation but helps the teeth immensely, preventing any teeth from growing crooked and ruining the mouth. Most vets will do this when the pup is six months old, but I try to leave it as late as possible, preferring it to be done at nine months.

After the removal of the canines and any other stubborn first teeth, and when the gums have healed and are no longer sore, clean the teeth every two or three days, using a dog toothpaste and baby brush. Taking the youngster's head, I gently rub the brush along the teeth. Do be gentle! They soon get used to their daily toiletry.

SOCIALISATION

Since the Yorkshire Terrier is such a sociable little character, socialisation presents few problems. Of all the breeds, the Yorkie is so adaptable that any situation is usually acceptable to him and gives him pleasure.

Once your new puppy has settled in his new home, invite friends to meet him. The Yorkie is not a shy dog, in spite of his size, and will approach any new situation with fearless confidence. If, from an early age, he associates human contact with a rewarding and enjoyable experience, he will grow up to be a well-rounded character, friendly to all.

A puppy that has been reared in the home will already be accustomed to human contact, everyday family life and ordinary household noises – the washing machine and vacuum cleaner etc. This may save considerable time overcoming any phobias at a later date.

When his vaccinations have been completed, take him on short trips to build up his confidence. Allow him to become familiar with new sights, smells and sounds, so that very little will surprise or unnerve him when he is an adult. You can also take him to a puppy training class to learn basic obedience, and to get him used to interacting with other dogs – of all shapes and sizes. The pups I have taken to such classes have hated it, but have loved general obedience training when they were a

little older – about six months of age.

Socialisation can take place anywhere. My young show prospects are taken to a playing field where they encounter the most intimidating of people – children. I let the children say 'hello' to the pup and pat him, as this certainly gives the pup a new confidence. Both the pup and the children look forward to these daily meetings. I had one veteran who ended up playing football (soccer) with the kids, and could dribble a ball with great skill.

CAR TRAVEL
Most Yorkies love the car – they love anything where they can be close to their family. A few react and will be car-sick. I ignore the sickness; I play music on the car radio, sing and be merry. Pander to his car sickness and your Yorkie will love the extra attention and

may never recover from his malady.

As the dog gets older, it is an excellent idea for him to travel in a crate or a carrying box. This is not only for his safety, but for yours, too, in case of an accident. Even a dog as small as a Yorkie can cause considerable damage if catapulted at speed during an emergency stop, or during a vehicle collision.

Training him to his crate or box is quite easy. For about a week, keep it in the lounge or kitchen and let him sit in it for regular short periods. Ignore the pitiful howling and reassure him. Praise him when he is quiet. Give him a tasty chew or a favourite toy to take his mind off being in the crate, and to make it seem a comfortable and enjoyable place to be. By the time he is ready to go in the crate in the car, he will be quite familiar with it and content to be there.

In my experience, Yorkies are great music-lovers, so having the radio or a tape on in the car may help to relax any nervous Yorkie passengers. If you sing, your Yorkie will usually join in. All my Champions have had their own tapes for travelling to shows – my current show prospect is a great fan of the Rolling Stones!

OLDER OR RESCUE DOG

An older dog can be a source of great pleasure. He has gone through his puppy days and probably comes pre-trained. You immediately see what you are getting, as his character is fully developed. You can assess him just as he will assess you, and you can both decide if you are made for each other.

You can acquire an older Yorkie through your nearest breed rescue organisation (contact your national Kennel Club for details). Many of these dogs are in rescue through no fault of their own. Every Yorkie I have rescued has been well-mannered and gentle. Many are a little sad at first, but with understanding, patience and love they soon rally round to their true Yorkie resilience.

Occasionally, a breeder may part with one of their older bitches. If you find

An older dog can be a marvellous addition to the family.

the training of a youngster rather daunting, this is an excellent alternative. A breeder who parts with an older dog is not necessarily cold-hearted or callous. They are thinking of the dog's welfare. Being so adaptable, she will soon settle in a new home and relish the idea of being an only child.

If deciding on an older Yorkie, ask why he is being rehomed. Where was he raised? Is he used to children or cats? Does he have a known medical history? This will all help to assess his suitability to your home and help you settle him into his new home if you do decide to take him on.

4 THE ADULT YORKIE

An adult Yorkie is a loyal and devoted friend. He is a very loving little character – brave and fearless, and full of fun and good humour. In today's world of flats and modern houses with small gardens, a Yorkie is the ideal pet: a big dog in a small package.

NUTRITION AND FEEDING

All dogs require a balanced diet to keep them healthy and to grow to their full potential, and your Yorkie will want it to be palatable. It is most important to feed him at the same time every day – dogs love routine, and irregular feeding times will upset his digestive system, possibly resulting in diarrhoea.

Because of his size, the Yorkshire Terrier requires quite a small amount of food. However, because of his high metabolic rate, a Yorkie can take a high-protein diet. You cannot risk letting a show dog, stud or brood bitch go off

their food. In my experience, the Yorkshire Terrier is one of the breeds that can literally forget to eat, especially when young, so you do have to pamper some of them.

My own Ch. Verolian Al Pacino was the most finicky of eaters as a youngster, sometimes going two or three days without food. This was very worrying, not only because he resembled a coat hanger, but also because he had no stamina to fight off any infection he might pick up at a dog show. After trying many remedies and cooking up numerous dishes for him, only to be ignored, I was finally advised to try Royal Jelly capsules. I gave him one in the morning and one at night and he was eating two meals a day within three days. Since then he has never looked back and has never had a day's illness. He was diagnosed as anorexic, but he was cured thanks to the bee.

The ideal pet – a big dog in a small package.

Photo: Carol Ann Johnson.

NUTRITIONAL NEEDS

Thanks to complete diets, all the work has been taken out of creating a balanced diet. If you give your dogs one meal of complete food a day, you can pamper to their fads for their second meal. Do use the products on the market today. A considerable amount of money has been used in research to produce these excellent products and, at the end of the day, you do know your dog has had the best: a complete balanced diet.

WATER

Earns its place at the top of the list since it is the most important nutrient, comprising 70 per cent of the lean, adult bodyweight. Your dog can survive after losing almost all of his fat and more than half of his protein stores. Daily water consumption, however, must be sufficient, since a loss of only 10 per cent of water will result in your dog's death.

Water does not supply energy or building blocks, but fulfils many other important functions and is necessary for life. Body tissues are between 70-90 per cent water and the presence of water within the body's tissues is essential for most chemical reactions.

Water is crucial for digestion, acts as a transport medium for nutrients and waste products, and absorbs heat from metabolic reactions so that there is little change in body temperature; it can transport heat away from working organs through the blood and dispense heat by evaporation in the form of sweat on the outer surface of the body.

Your Yorkie experiences daily water loss via the faeces and urine, so his water intake must compensate for this. His water requirement is obtained from three sources:

Metabolic water – produced from the breakdown of proteins, fats and carbohydrates, supplying only 5-10 per cent of his daily water intake.

Water from food – derived from ingested food; this can vary from 8 per cent to as much as 80 per cent moisture.

Drinking water – the sum total of water derived from the first two sources will then determine the actual amount your Yorkie drinks from his bowl. It is very important to have fresh clean water available always. His water requirement will increase with the environmental temperature and level of exercise.

A balanced diet is an essential factor in preserving good health.

Photo: Carol Ann Johnson.

PROTEIN

Protein has many functions in your Yorkie's metabolism. It is continuously required to replace muscle, skin and coat and is required in the form of enzymes and hormones. It can also be used as an energy source, although it provides less than half the number of calories per gram compared to fat.

The building blocks of protein are known as amino acids and these are supplied to your Yorkie once the protein source is broken down and absorbed across the intestinal wall. There are 20 amino acids commonly found in nature and they can be thought of as different letters in the alphabet. They are put together in specific combinations to give us the wide diversity of words, or, in this case, proteins that the animal will require.

FAT

Fat is required for many functions in your Yorkie's metabolism, the most significant being as an energy provider and as a source of essential fatty acids, such as linoleic acid.

Once broken down, fat will supply your dog with approximately double the amount of calories per gram, compared to protein and carbohydrate. The fat content of a diet also enhances palatability, which is a very important factor to consider when feeding your Yorkie.

Fat can be split into vegetable oils and animal fats (oils being liquid at room temperature, fats being solid). All vegetable oils are deficient in arachidonic acid, which is an essential fatty acid. Animal fats generally have a higher and more consistent level of essential fatty acids compared to vegetable oils. Animal fats themselves vary in quality – chicken fat is considered to be the highest-quality fat source available. The first clinical sign of a fatty acid deficiency will be scaly, flaky skin and a coarse dull coat.

CARBOHYDRATE

When dogs lived in the wild, their original diet of a carcass consisted primarily of protein and fat – the only carbohydrate ingested would have been the semi-digested material in the gut of the prey. When considering the optimum nutrition for your Yorkie, a source of carbohydrate should be included as it is an efficient source of glucose; it is also a source of energy, but, only offering half the calories per gram compared to fat, it is regarded as an inefficient energy source. Common sources include: rice, wheat, oats and corn, and biscuit. Carbohydrates fed in bulk would indicate an inferior quality diet.

VITAMINS

These can be split into two catergories:
• Water-soluble, which includes the B-complex and vitamin C. If fed in excess, they will be excreted in the urine.
• Fat-soluble vitamins include A, D, E,

and K. Usually found in the liver, these vitamins can potentially be stored anywhere in the body where fat is present. They can be toxic and should be fed in small amounts. Vitamin C is the only vitamin produced by your Yorkie's body, so others must be supplied in his diet. They are essential for his normal metabolic functioning, to help in his resistance against disease and infection.

Remember to consult your vet if you are in any doubt about vitamin dosage – far more problems occur from owners oversupplementing than undersupplementing.

The vitamins required for a balanced diet are:

• **Vitamin A** – found in fish liver oil, animal liver, milk, eggs, green vegetables. Lack of this vitamin can cause hair to become dry and fall out, faulty dentition and bone structure, and lack of development.

• **Vitamin B1** – found in brewer's yeast, rice, liver, lean pork and brown whole-wheat bread. Lack of this vitamin can cause poor appetite and poor nervous system, and the digestive system can suffer.

• **Vitamin B2** – called the red vitamin, and found in liver and kidneys. Fresh muscle meat rich in this vitamin is very good in cases of anaemia.

• **Vitamin D** – found in sterilised bone meal, milk, yolk of egg, fish oil. This vitamin prevents rickets. Good for the correct bone structure and good sound teeth.

• **Vitamin E** – found in wheatgerm oil. Supposedly prevents sterility, and helps in coordination of the nervous system.

MINERALS
These are inorganic compounds, and include calcium, magnesium, sodium and potassium.

Only four per cent of your Yorkie's total body weight is comprised of mineral matter, but it is essential to life. Minerals play a vital role in the formation of structural components, such as bones and teeth – 99 per cent of the body's calcium is found in the skeleton. They also maintain the body-fluid balance and act as catalysts for metabolic reactions.

TYPES OF FOOD

There are many types of prepared dog foods on the market.

Tinned foods
There are many proprietary brands of dog food in tins for the toy dog, and most are welcomed with relish. My Robert (Ch. Verolian Justajule) could pick out a tin of his favourite brand of dog food from a tin of beans, a tomato

tin and a tin of stewed steak, often performing this party trick for my disbelieving friends. He never got it wrong. Most – though not all – tinned foods are not complete diets and require a mixer.

Complete foods

Too numerous to list. Each is a complete, balanced diet and extremely practical, being clean and easy to use. There are two basic types. One type contains red and white meat and is made up with brown rice and barley. In this type, the bulk tends to be higher, so you provide slightly more food per body weight of dog. A good eater will do well on this type. The other type is made from fresh chicken meat, with little bulking material. This type of food should be given in smaller amounts, since 85 per cent of the nutrition is readily absorbed. Most of these products are gluten-free, and ingredients vary, so do check the packaging.

Fresh meat

In my opinion, this is one of the best ways to feed a Toy dog, especially the brood bitch, stud dog or show dog. However, it can be expensive. Remember also that meat alone is not giving your dog a balanced diet, so he should have his diet supplemented – perhaps with a vitamin pill. Ask your vet to advise you.

I use minced (chopped) beef from the butcher, cooked with carrot, potato and any green vegetable. This makes a welcome change during the cold winter months. I give liver once a week. Never boil it, as it can go through them and give them diarrhoea. Fry it in a little butter instead. I give my dog green tripe (offal) regularly, the finely chopped and washed kind. Chicken is also received with relish, but the dogs are often reluctant to return to their normal diet. I'm sure we create problems by obeying their fads.

The type of feeding method you use is largely a matter of personal choice.

Photo: Steve Nash.

Other products

There are many other products available, too. It is worth trying different types of food until you find one that is ideal for your individual dog. On the market nowadays are many rolls of meat, similar to large sausages. Or you can try small foil packs, which are easy, convenient and always eaten with enthusiasm. Some are especially prepared for the smaller dog and these are generally greeted with relish.

Mixers and biscuits

Mixers usually make the dog's meal balanced when used with tinned meat.

Dog biscuits come in a variety of sizes and colours, even hypo-allergenic biscuits are available, so dogs with food allergies need not miss out on their daily treats. Biscuits probably supply your Yorkie with enough of the carbohydrate needed in his diet, giving him some fibre too. Some biscuits claim to keep your dog's teeth healthy and free from tartar. Biscuits can also have great entertainment value – Yorkies can spend hours playing with their biscuits.

Biscuit meal can be mixed with fresh meat to supply some nutrients, but do not feed too much, as bulk feeding is not necessary for a Yorkie. With this diet, he must be given a vitamin and mineral supplement.

Bones

Do be careful if you give bones to your Yorkie, as they can splinter. If swallowed in this state, they can cause serious damage, and can even be fatal; so check and replace bones regularly. I only give bones to my dogs when I can keep a close eye on them. If you have more than one Yorkie, remember that bones can cause squabbles.

Treats

Do give treats as a reward, but do not give too many. Yorkies are small, and giving too many treats may mean your dog will not eat his main meal.

Milk

On no account give a Yorkie cow's milk; it causes diarrhoea. If you must give milk, only give goat's milk or a milk supplement for puppies (such as Lactol). I start to wean my pups on Lactol and have one 14-month-old who still loves her Lactol drink in the morning.

QUANTITIES OF FOOD

This depends on the dog. Like people, some dogs require larger amounts than others. A greedy dog needs a controlled diet. As the owner, it is for you to decide how much each dog needs. I have a one-pound girl who eats as much as a five-pound girl; the second is as fat as butter, but the first is still quite lean. You will have to regulate and decide the quantities according to your dog's needs and metabolic rate.

Do be careful not to overfeed your dog. Being a domesticated dog, your

Yorkshire Terrier does not exercise as much as a wild dog in its primitive state. As a result, his weight must be watched or else he will become too fat, which could affect his heart and shorten his life.

FOOD ALLERGIES

It would appear food allergies are much more common nowadays. Allergic reactions often manifest themselves in skin problems. If you suspect your Yorkie has a food allergy, consult a vet who will be able to test and diagnose the food that is responsible. An exclusion diet will be the first step. This is where individual foods or ingredients are eliminated from the diet: if the dog improves when not being fed a certain food, you will probably have found the culprit.

Dogs can be allergic to any type of food. Beef, soya, wheat and wheat gluten (corn and corn gluten), egg and dairy products have all been known to cause allergic and digestive problems in some dogs. If your Yorkie is allergic to a type of food, you should feed a hypo-allergenic food, usually a complete feed made only from pure, natural ingredients like rice (easily digested), oats for energy, linseed for a glossy, healthy coat, seaweed for nutrients, and turkey or lamb. Your vet will be able to advise you further.

EXERCISE

Whatever diet you decide to give your dog, remember that, without exercise, your Yorkie will not be fit. I look on my Yorkies as athletes, fit in mind and body, and try to keep them in this condition.

Being a country dweller, I am fortunate to be able to give the Yorkies walks across fields. Usually a lead is not necessary, since we never encounter other dogs on our walks. Free-running is very enjoyable for the dogs; they are able to go and seek new smells, chase a rabbit, or just keep on my heels in case I should disappear! The Yorkies cover much more ground than I do, and their free-running exercise keeps their minds alert and bodies fit.

The quantity you feed varies enormously according to the individual.
Photo: Steve Nash.

Do not make the mistake of thinking that a Toy dog does not require exercise. Photo: Amanda Bulbeck.

Even my show dogs, done up in crackers (wraps), loves these walks – jumping puddles, racing over a ploughed field, and taking in the wildlife smells. This builds muscle and keeps their brains alert so the dog is interested in all his outings, show or otherwise.

You should integrate some road-walking in your exercise routine as it helps to keep the dog's nails short and offers a little variety.

If you live in a town, you should either give your Yorkie a couple of walks in a park, or plenty of free-running and playing in the garden (if it is large enough). If you visit the country with your town Yorkie, be aware that he is in strange territory. With lots of new smells around, he could possibly run off, ignoring your calls. Never let your dog off the lead when sheep are about; extending leads are ideal for these forays.

After a period of bad weather, or if you have not been able to get out much, build up the length of your dog's exercise gradually, gently increasing the walk. I find this very important with an older dog who will tire more quickly than a younger one – though the joy of having a small dog, is that he can easily be carried home if you feel he has had enough exercise.

These little dogs have great stamina and are quite capable of walking ten miles or more if in good physical shape. If time does not permit a long walk, make sure the dog gets suitable exercise in the garden. Yorkies love to run and grab their special toys, and will do this exercise far longer than you anticipated. I have one girl who loves to play football with the downfalls from the apple trees; she plays this game for hours and is very fit!

I have never found Yorkies to be particularly fond of water or indeed of swimming, though there are always exceptions. On the odd occasion when one of my Yorkies has fallen in, the miserable wet creature could not wait to escape.

NEUTERING

Neutering is the removal of the reproductive parts of a male or female. It should not alter the temperament or character of the dog or bitch. Neutering can have the effect of thickening the coat, and some dogs can be inclined to put on weight, so they will need monitoring and their diets adjusted accordingly.

Neutering is a personal matter. I know of many pet owners who abhor the idea of it. If you feel it is right for your lifestyle, especially where a female is concerned, go ahead – you will be preventing unwanted litters and will not be altering your dog's temperament in any way.

A female Yorkie comes into season every six to ten months; some can be later, having a year between seasons. When in season, the bitch will bleed for up to 12 days, causing stains on the furniture. Dogs will find your bitch irresistible while she is in heat, so, for the three weeks of her season, you should keep her indoors.

It can be dangerous if your Yorkie mates an unsuitable dog: if he is considerably larger than her (as most dogs are, in relation to the Yorkie), she could produce large puppies which she is unable to give birth to, resulting in a Caesarean. And, again due to her size, it could be near impossible for her to rear the pups, taking all her body resources, and this could result in eclampsia and poor health generally. The other disadvantage is that crossbreed litters can be more difficult to find homes for.

If your bitch should get mated accidently, there is an injection which the vet can give that halts the pregnancy. You have about 24 hours to have this injection administered.

A male will show signs of his sexual prowess from six months to a year, depending on his size. I have found smaller males slower to mature sexually, though some mature later than others, irrespective of size.

A male will show interest in sex from his early months. He will start to lift his leg when he urinates, and may start 'humping' favourite toys. With a firm "No", you can nip this unsociable activity in the bud. Some females will take up this activity too, even those that have been neutered. This may be because 'humping' can be a sign of dominance over another dog.

VETERAN CARE

There is nothing more delightful than an old Yorkie, tongue hanging out, completely set in his ways and demanding your love constantly. He has been your constant companion and part of the family from puppyhood to 10 years or more; now his loyalty and devotion deserve your special attention. Most Yorkies do not incur huge veterinary bills throughout their lives; but expect to spend a little money on your ageing Yorkie; he's worth it.

The body is now ageing, the organs are functioning less efficiently, and sight and hearing may lose their keenness. This does not necessarily mean you have to change your Yorkie's normal routine but, if you recognise any symptoms of ageing, adjust the lifestyle accordingly. You should keep your dog scrupulously clean, and should regulate his exercise and diet (he will require less protein).

The ageing Yorkie can either put on weight; or may have a tendency towards being lean. If your dog is prone to weight gain, his diet should be adjusted accordingly by reducing the fat content. As he starts to exercise less, his food could be cut down further. Always cut his food down gradually, and, if he appears ravenous, split his meals into two. With a lean dog, you can pander to his fancies.

Symptoms of old age can spread over a couple of years, some dogs showing no changes at all. However, look out for drier hair, a sparse coat that's lost something of the shine of youth, dry skin, and possible blindness or deafness; all these can result from old age. All Yorkies love warmth, and now it becomes more important as the internal functions no longer respond in the same way to heat, cold and exercise. It is important to pander to your Yorkie's whims.

In addition, there may be growths, heart problems, prostates (inflammation of the prostate gland), pyometra (infection of the womb), or nephritis (kidney infection). The reassurance is that today's veterinary medicine can successfully treat many afflictions from which the ageing dog may suffer, and many old Yorkies show no sign of these conditions.

He may need to be groomed a little more regularly, as it will stimulate his skin and keep his coat looking good. You should also do regular checks on teeth.

Mentally, your dog needs reassurance as his physical vitality declines. He tries fiercely to hold on to his familiar world, retaining his stability and mental health. When he comes to you for attention, lavish love and affection on your old friend.

If, at this stage, you introduce a young puppy into the household, reassure your oldie constantly that he stands first in your affections. Do this by plenty of play and patting, doing everything possible to make the last years as rewarding as the early ones. Often the arrival of a young puppy gives the old Yorkie a new lease of life, although you should also ensure your veteran gets sufficient sleep and rest from the newcomer.

Any traumatic occurrence can affect your ageing Yorkie, and he could literally give up the will to live if he thought you had deserted him, thinking he had outlived his purpose. It is vital for his daily routine to continue as always, with your devoted love.

It is a good idea to take your Yorkie to the vet for six-monthly check-ups and, if you suspect any ailment, to consult a vet immediately.

Ch. Verolian Temptress At Ozmilion:
Sprightly and alert at 12 years of age.
Photo: Russell Fine Art.

Hopefully, your dog will go through his later years with the minimum of trouble, giving you continued pleasure. These years should be your best, because your Yorkie is an old friend, loyal and devoted.

EUTHANASIA

It is your duty to know when it is time to put your Yorkie to sleep. This is the saddest time of pet ownership, but you owe it to your dog to ensure he does not suffer unnecessarily. This is the kindest act you can do for your Yorkie.

Coping with the loss of a pet can be very difficult. Children may find it particularly traumatic, and elderly owners may feel isolated by the loss. Do not be embarrassed to grieve, make sure you rely on the support of family and friends to see you through this difficult time. Remember that other animals in the house may be affected, too.

As time passes, a new puppy or dog may be the answer, but never look for your old pal in them, as they are all individuals.

5 HEALTH CARE

Fortunately, Yorkshire Terriers are not prone to the scourges of many other breeds. However, there is always the exception, and naturally accidents can and do happen. For this reason, all possible precautions should be taken.

Do not let your Yorkie jump off any height, such as the sofa or the bed, as he can jar his joints, especially if he is not fully grown. Some Yorkies become great leapers, and are quite capable of clearing 18 inches to two feet in one bound, so be vigilant. You should also be careful when your Yorkie is picked up by visitors. He will be very excited to greet any guests, and, if picked up, his excited wriggling could mean he falls.

Yorkies love to investigate, and delight in rummaging through cupboards. Keep all your cleaning materials and other hazardous items well out of your dog's reach. This also applies to insecticides and chemicals in the garden shed.

Make your garden safe, too. Check with your garden centre what plants are dangerous for dogs, and make sure your Yorkie cannot escape through any gaps in your garden's fencing.

With the high cost of veterinary bills it is well worth considering pet insurance. The breeder may even have insured the pup already.

FINDING A GOOD VET
Consult your local phone directory and ring any vets in your area to find out if they are sympathetic to Toy dogs. Each vet is different, and some do not seem to like tiny dogs. Recommendation is the best policy. If the vet has a good reputation, you are half-way there.

The vet should inspire much confidence: during your Yorkie's life, the vet's care could mean life and death to your little dog, so you must have full trust in the vet's ability.

Never be afraid to ask questions about your dog's treatment.

Fortunately, the Yorkshire Terrier is a hardy little dog and most will experience few major health problems.

Photo: Carol Ann Johnson.

COMMON AILMENTS

ANAL GLANDS

You will find these glands on each side of the anus, situated inside and below. They secrete a yellowish fluid, necessary for scent-marking. Occasionally, these glands can accumulate the secretion, which is usually emptied during defecation. They become itchy as they overfill, causing your dog to drag his bottom on the ground, or even to nibble his rear end. Your vet will be able to empty the glands for you, and show you how to do it in future.

BITES

The canines of any dog are long and punishing. One bite can inject an infection straight into the victim. Any dog bite suffered by your Yorkie needs instant bathing. If the bites are serious, you should contact your vet, as there could be a risk of internal injuries. The vet will stitch the bite, if necessary, and may give an antibiotic injection to prevent any infection.

If you suspect your dog has been bitten by a snake, you should contact your vet at once.

BROKEN BONES

A Yorkie's front legs seem very susceptible to breaking (particularly when he is a puppy), so avoid boisterous play and rough handling, especially by children.

If an injury does occur, the dog will cry in pain, the affected leg will hang limply, and there will be swelling and inflammation in the vicinity of the fracture. The dog may go into shock and must have veterinary help immediately; if there is any delay, try to reduce the dog's pain by making him comfortable and keeping him warm. Be careful not to damage the limb further.

CANINE DISTEMPER

This is a virus infection that attacks the dog's tissues, particularly through the mucous membranes. The best method of prevention is vaccination.

If your Yorkie should develop this

dreadful disease, immediate veterinary treatment is required, as distemper can be a killer. Symptoms include: a running nose, a dry cough, and loss of appetite. The dog's bowels may be loose and his eyes may have a discharge. He may be miserable and depressed.

As the disease progresses, the symptoms will get worse, and your Yorkie is likely to sleep a lot. He will become dehydrated, and will develop a great thirst. The discharge from his eyes and nose may become thicker, and he may develop pimples with pus in the abdominal area. A great deal of nursing care is required. You will have to keep his nose and eyes clear of the thick mucus. You may also have to adjust his diet to encourage him to eat. Your vet should be able to advise you.

A dog that has had distemper can be left with yellow teeth where the enamel has deteriorated; this is known as 'distemper teeth'. The vaccination may also cause this condition.

CONVALESCENT CARE

A sick Yorkie requires quiet and rest. Knowing no limits to his energy, he will try to take part in all the surrounding activities, but you should restrict his activity so he doesn't overdo it. If your dog has been hospitalised, he will return home with a routine to follow, which must be followed to the letter. Sympathy, love, and familiar surroundings will improve his morale and recovery time.

DENTAL PROBLEMS

As in all Toy breeds, in which a small jaw has to accommodate many teeth, tartar can build up very quickly, leading to bad breath, gum recession and bacterial infection. Heart trouble can result, especially in an older dog, if it is left untreated.

Dogs do not ordinarily develop cavities, but will accumulate brown tartar on their teeth.

As a puppy, a Yorkie will cut his baby (milk) teeth by ten weeks of age, 32 in all. At five to six months, he will start to shed these milk teeth and get his permanent set of 42.

During this transition, some of the milk teeth can refuse to budge, especially the baby canines. In bad cases, a double row of teeth may be evident.

During teething, your Yorkie's gums will be red and swollen, and he will want to chew. A chew or hard toy will relieve some of the discomfort, and will help the milk teeth to loosen and fall out. If the milk teeth are left, tartar will build up quickly on both sets of teeth, especially the large, permanent canines.

If this is the case, a visit to your vet is a must, as the offending milk teeth will have to be removed.

During a veterinary dental, the vet will remove all tartar under anaesthetic and polish the dog's teeth. Cleaning your dog's teeth from an early age will save this expense and will keep your dog healthy.

ENTERITIS (inflammation of the intestine)
Diarrhoea, often containing mucus, is the main symptom of this condition. It can be temporary or chronic, attacking only a small section of small intestine. Your dog may assume a crouched position. You may even hear noises coming from his stomach region. A bland diet is required, such as rice and white meat. If there is no improvement, a vet must be consulted.

EYE PROBLEMS
CERF (Certified Eye Registry Foundation) is the registry in the US that certifies eye health, and many breeders also have their breeding stock certified by CERF. Yorkies are not particularly prone to eye diseases, but some have suffered from Progressive Retinal Atrophy and Juvenile Cataracts, both of which seem to be hereditary.

FLEAS
These little parasites can cause havoc with a Yorkie's coat, and the show specimen should be free of them at all costs. Fleas will make your dog scratch furiously. In time, his coat will be destroyed, along with his skin.

Some Yorkies are so sensitive to fleas that they can develop chronic parasitic dermatitis.

Many excellent products are available to eradicate fleas. All bedding should be washed regularly, and vacuuming will remove any eggs, especially in a kennel.

GASTRITIS (inflammation of the stomach wall)
The main symptom is vomiting after eating or drinking. The dog may even feel pain when his stomach is touched. In many cases, starving for 24 hours does the trick. If the dog appears thirsty, an ice cube may be given, but do not let him gulp liquid quickly from a bowl, as he may not be able to keep it down. In severe cases, a vet must be consulted, since the dog may become dehydrated which is very dangerous in a small Yorkie. With proper care, he should soon bounce back to proper health.

HEART DISEASE
As your Yorkie approaches old age, he may develop a heart disorder. There is no specific heartbeat rate for dogs, but Toy dogs have a higher rate per minute than large dogs. Symptoms include: a hacking, dry cough; blue discoloration of the gums and tongue; becoming winded or gasping for breath; loss of vitality; and tiring easily. Follow your vet's advice. With modern methods and new medicines, heart disorders can be treated successfully.

KENNEL COUGH
This is a very infectious disease caused by two viruses: Bordetella and Parainfluenza. They both affect the dog's trachea and lungs, causing him to cough hoarsely. Some dogs will cough for weeks, others may cough only once. Sometimes there may be a discharge of

pus from the eyes and nose.

This disease used to be very common in kennels, especially boarding kennels. Being an air-borne virus, it can be easily transmitted from one dog to another.

When your Yorkie has his first vaccinations, ask your vet if it includes protection for the Parainfluenza virus. Most vaccines include this today. A separate vaccine is needed for the Bordetella virus, where drops are administered down the nose. It is essential to ensure your dog is protected if he is due to go into boarding kennels.

LEGGE PERTHES DISEASE
This is a congenital disease not only common in dogs but also in humans. It occurs when the blood supply to the hip joint is blocked, resulting in deterioration of the joint, which can necessitate surgery. In humans, it is often found in teenage children, and has been known to right itself within a couple of years, the blood supply returning to the joint and the hip being quite normal.

A dog with the disease will rather sit than stand, and can show discomfort. As with humans, the disease usually develops at about 10-12 months.

LEPTOSPIROSIS
This is an infectious disease of humans and dogs, and some other mammals. The disease can be contracted through water which may be infected with rat urine, which spreads the disease. Keep your Yorkie away from rat-infested water or river banks, and do not leave drinking bowls outdoors overnight. If you have rats on, or passing through, your property, they must be removed.

The disease is caused by living organisms called Leptospira. There are three that are of the greatest importance, although there are many species found worldwide. The three types we are concerned with are:
• L. Icterohemorrhagiae – causes jaundice. It is carried by rats whose infected urine spreads the disease
• L. Canicola – results in nephritis (kidney disease) in dogs and humans, and can develop into meningitis in people. Carried mainly by dogs, it is spread by an infected animal through the urine. Can also infect cats, cattle and foxes.
• L. Pomona – causes fever and kidney disease. Carried in cows, pigs, dogs and humans. Infection can occur after swimming in infected water.

The bacteria are able to permeate through unbroken skin, where, by simply dividing, they will multiply, and infect and destroy body cells and tissue, especially the liver and kidneys. It will then pass out of the dog's body and be passed on to other animals.

The onset of this disease is sudden, and symptoms include: loss of appetite, bright orange urine, rise in temperature, vomiting, abdominal discomfort, jaundice and diarrhoea.

There is a high fatality rate in young dogs. A convalescence period of one or two weeks is required for a dog to make a full recovery, because of the damage to his digestive system, liver, and kidneys. The treatment for Leptospirosis is an intense course of antibiotics.

Your Yorkie should have a Leptospirosis vaccine when a puppy, followed by yearly boosters.

MANGE MITES

Mange is a serious skin disease. Not only does it cause discomfort, but it can also lead to serious complications.

Demodectic mange mites are cigar-shaped parasites that spread rapidly over the dog's body, resulting in infections wherever they go.

Sarcoptic mange mites, spider-shaped parasites, cause scabs and inflammation on the body, resulting in hair loss. The dog may also smell sour, and these mites can be transmitted to humans.

Prevention is better than cure: the dog that is washed, brushed and combed regularly will not pick up any parasitic infestation. Your veterinary surgeon will recommend powders, dips, or sprays to eliminate the parasites infesting your dog.

Otodectic mange infests the dog's ear. As a result, the dog carries his head at a strange angle and the ear discharges a brown, smelly fluid. The condition can be kept at bay by regular cleaning of the ear with a proprietary ear lotion.

MICROVASCULAR DYSPLASIA

A recent health concern has been the rising incidence of Microvascular Dysplasia (a small-sized liver) in the US. There are few definitive tests which can be carried out on pups to determine if they have this condition. DNA tests may be developed in the next few years to identify carriers.

PARVOVIRUS

This is every breeder's nightmare, and was the scourge of the later 70s and early 80s. It is a tenacious virus spread from dog to dog – either through faeces, or via clothing, footwear and anything else that may have been in contact with an infected dog. Infection occurs by the ingestion of virus particles, and, after an outbreak, can remain viable in the house for up to a year. Parvovirus is very difficult to eradicate, and resists many disinfectants, but strong bleach can help to kill it.

There are two strains:
- **Canine parvovirus myocarditis** concentrates on the heart muscle of new-born puppies which are exposed to it. The effect usually takes from four to ten weeks, and apparently normal, healthy pups in the litter will suddenly collapse and die. Some do survive. Any breeding bitch should be vaccinated to provide some antibodies to the infection through her milk.
- **Intestinal parvovirus** is the most common type, and can attack a dog of any age, usually proving fatal in the pup.

Symptoms include: complete lethargy, loss of appetite, vomiting and diarrhoea (often with a blood content), and severe abdominal pain (which can appear similar to severe enteritis). From the onset of infection, the dog can be dead within five days, dying in considerable pain. Those that survive will show a noticeable improvement within this time. Fatalities are often due to dehydration, so an intravenous drip is often required to replace fluid loss.

Any house or kennel that contracts this infectious disease should avoid all other dogs. Isolating the sick dog can help to contain it. Vaccination should protect your dog against canine parvovirus – first when a pup and then as a yearly booster.

PATELLA LUXATION (slipping patella)
This is quite common in most Toy breeds, the Yorkshire Terrier being no exception. The patella is a small bone which lies in a groove at the lower end of the thigh bone. When the dog bends the knee joint, it slides along the groove. If the groove is too shallow, it will slip out to one side, causing the dog to go lame. It may be so bad, that the leg is useless and the dog walks on three legs or takes two or three strides and hops. Severe cases require an operation. Affected animals should not be bred from.

Knee (and hip) certification are becoming more popular among breeders. OFA (Orthopedic Foundation for Animals) is the certifying registry for both patella X-rays and hip X-rays.

PORTOSYSTEMIC SHUNT
Portosystemic Shunt (PSS) in the breed is on the increase in the US. Unfortunately at this time there are few definitive tests that can be performed on young puppies to determine whether or not either of these conditions are present. A portogram (where dye is injected into the portal vein to see whether blood flows through the liver or outside of it) can be used to determine the presence of a shunt, but this is invasive surgery and the puppy must be sedated.

Radio-Scintigraphy is another test that can be performed but this test must usually be done at a Veterinary University. The Yorkie must be hospitalised for several days following the procedure as radioactive dyes are injected which then require special handling of all waste products. It is hoped within the next few years that a DNA test can be used which would identify carriers of the problems who can then be eliminated from breeding programmes. The Yorkshire Terrier Club of America Foundation, Inc. was formed in 1991 to raise research money to study PSS and microvascular dysplasia.

Diet is an important part of treatment for shunt. Protein is very difficult to tolerate and thus dogs with shunt should be fed low-protein diets.

PROSTATITIS
The prostate gland may become enlarged in older male dogs. This causes loss of

appetite, pain and possibly a reluctance to sit down due to the inflamed gland. Veterinary help must be sought. Hormone injections will probably return your dog to normal health. The hormones used are female, so don't expect your boy to be interested in the opposite sex for a while! If this fails, surgery on the prostate is performed.

PYOMETRA

This is an accumulation of pus in the uterus, which may be open or closed. Open pyometra is obvious from the discharge from the uterus, which can be thick and greenish or red, as though the bitch is in continual heat. She may give off a sickly, sweetish odour. Closed pyometra is apparent from the distended abdomen, pain and general sickliness. Both are accompanied by thirst, increased urination, vomiting, temperature rise and loss of appetite. Veterinary help is required immediately. Vets generally try antibiotics first, but a complete hysterectomy is usually required.

RABIES

This must be one of the most feared diseases, as it can be passed on to humans. Not all bites from a rabid animal develop into rabies in the recipient, but if the virus does develop, there is no recovery and death is the inevitable outcome.

Rabies is a disease of the nervous system. The virus is transmitted in the saliva of a rabid animal, usually as a result of a bite, although it can also be transmitted by saliva entering a lesion in the skin. Once the virus enters the body, it is transmitted to the nervous tissue and eventually on to the brain, where it causes an inflammation called encephalitis.

Once the brain is inflamed, a dog's behaviour will change in one of two ways. He may become lethargic, depressed and incapable of action, his lower jaw hanging as if useless, the tongue drooling saliva. Or he may be overexcited, or what is called 'furious', in his behaviour, being irritated by, chasing, and attacking, anything that moves. He will be anxious and his pupils will probably be dilated.

The dog will also have great difficulty swallowing, the virus eventually paralysing the nerves of the throat and the jaw muscles. Rabies was known as hydrophobia (fear of water), but the dog is not actually frightened of the water; rather, he is alarmed by the fact he has a great thirst and is unable to swallow. Eventually, the dog will become paralysed, go into a coma, and die. Dogs seldom survive more than 15 days from the first signs of the disease.

Vaccines should be given in countries where rabies is present. Currently, the UK does not require such a vaccine because the country is protected by quarantine. With a new pet passport system shortly being introduced, however, this situation will change.

Rabies vaccinations are required in most states of the US, on an annual or bi-annual basis. The virus is carried by bats, raccoons, skunks and foxes; even in the most urban areas, skunks and raccoons sometimes make their appearance, so it is wise to have the Yorkie's shots current and up to date.

RINGWORM

No worm is involved in ringworm; it is a fungal infection. The name is derived from the oval lesions appearing on the skin, which grow larger as the infection spreads. A vet can identify ringworm and treat it appropriately with washes, injections or drugs. It can be transmitted to humans.

SHOCK

A dog who has been in an accident or a dog fight may suffer from shock. He will appear to be asleep or semi-conscious, the gums and inside of the lips may appear whitish, and the breathing will be rapid and shallow. The body temperature will be low and, since the muscles relax during shock, the dog will have no control over his bladder and bowels.

It is an extremely serious condition and must be treated immediately. Raise the temperature by wrapping the dog in blankets, with a hot-water bottle. Keep the dog quiet and reassure him; holding him, or sitting and soothing him, may help to maintain his will to live. If the dog is fully conscious and can swallow, small amounts of fluid, such as warm glucose water, will prevent dehydration. If veterinary help is sought, on no account leave your Yorkie; in this state, he may think you have deserted him and may die.

STINGS

Bee and wasp stings cause considerable pain – your Yorkie is likely to cry out and rush around. If he has been stung on the face, he may paw and shake his head.

You should discourage your dog from snapping at insects, as a sting in the mouth can be dangerous. The area around the sting will swell, and, if this is in the mouth, it can cut off your dog's airways. If you suspect your dog has been stung in the mouth, you should seek immediate veterinary treatment.

Bee stings should be removed with tweezers and the area bathed in bicarbonate of soda. Apply vinegar to wasp stings. An antihistamine injection may be needed if your dog has a serious reaction to the sting.

TICKS

Ticks are easily recognised. They look like flat, blackish-brown seeds, and can also give the appearance of small warts. There is a little tick-removing device on the market which removes the entire organism. The tick's head must always be removed, otherwise it will remain in the skin and can develop into an abscess. There are many products available to eradicate ticks. Smothering the tick in Vaseline (pharmacy grade petroleum jelly) will cause it eventually to drop off.

If you should walk your Yorkie through a sheep-grazing field, there is a good chance he will pick up a tick. Immature ticks rest on shrubs and grasses, waiting for a host to pass by. If your dog brushes past, the tick will drop on to the dog to obtain the blood meal it requires to complete its life-cycle.

A serious infestation may mean your dog becomes anaemic – his gums may appear pale. In some countries, (e.g. America and Australia), tick bites can be very serious, transmitting diseases, such as Lymes Disease and Tularemia (an infectious disease of rodents, transmitted to man by infected ticks), to humans. Shots for both humans and animals to protect against Lymes Disease have been put on the market very recently in America.

VACCINATION
Today, the terrible diseases of distemper (hardpad), hepatitis, leptospirosis, parvovirus and parainfluenza can all be controlled by vaccination. This makes the dog immune to the diseases. Outside the UK, rabies jabs may also be necessary. The puppy usually starts his course of vaccinations between 8 and 12 weeks; an annual booster is generally recommended.

WORMS
Dogs should be wormed regularly (follow your vet's advice on dosage and frequency). A dog with worms is listless and has a bloated stomach and a dry, coarse coat. Loss of weight is apparent and bowel motions are thin. If you are in doubt, the vet will quickly determine what worm is involved and prescribe the correct treatment.

There are several types of worm. The most common is the roundworm or ascarid – a white, slim worm, about one to four inches in length, which develops in the intestine. It is very common in puppies and can affect the unborn puppy.

It is common for a worm infestation to cause dogs to hiccup. In severe cases, the dog may have convulsions.

Regular worming is essential for adults and puppies; your vet will advise you on dosages. Any bitch should be wormed prior to mating, then again within the last 14 days preceding her whelping.

Your dog's faeces should be picked up and disposed of properly, and all members of the household should wash their hands regularly, especially after handling the dog. Babies and young dogs should be prevented from sucking the dog's toys.

The tapeworm is flat, segmented and can measure up to 20 inches in length. There are two types: Dipylidium, which spends part of its cycle in the flea (the dog has to swallow the flea to become infected), and Taenia, which spends part of its life-cycle in the rabbit or mouse (the dog must eat part of their intestines to become infected).

The head (of both types) attaches to the intestinal lining, where it grows, becoming longer and longer. Some of the segments eventually break off and will appear in the faeces or around the anus, looking like grains of rice. Severe infestation will cause diarrhoea and poor growth in puppies.

Heartworms are parasites transmitted to the dog through the mosquito bite. The larvae are deposited on the dog's skin and will eventually burrow into a vein. They migrate to the heart, where they can live for several years, preventing the natural flow of blood and finally causing heart failure.

If infected with the heartworm, the dog will tire easily, lose weight, and will cough. A blood test will confirm the presence of this worm. Treatment can include regular medication or surgery to remove the worm.

Heartworms are not found in the UK, except in the occasional imported dogs and quarantine kennel. Heartworm exists in most parts of the US now, and, because it is mosquito-borne, dogs in warmer climates are usually given heartworm medication year round. There are several different types of heartworm medication: a daily tablet, a monthly dosage, some are chewable, some are not, these are usually wrapped in a piece of cheese or meat to make it palatable for the Yorkie.

Other worms include hook and whip worms. Both are very serious and can be fatal in a pup. They are not very common, usually infecting only dogs kept in grass runs, and are very rare in the Yorkshire Terrier because of his lifestyle. The hookworm larvae invade the skin, resulting in dermatitis between the toes. The larvae are then ingested by the dog and will hook on to the intestinal wall. They live on blood, and can cause the dog to become anaemic and have blood-streaked faeces.

Whipworm (roundish and tapered in shape) is also ingested, but as an egg. It settles in the colon, where it multiplies and causes chronic diarrhoea, loss of blood and discomfort.

Both hookworm and whipworm are difficult to diagnose. If you suspect your dog has either of these worms, consult your vet – who may have to analyse one of your dog's stools. Strict hygiene methods and regular worming are essential to prevent worm infestation.

WOUNDS

Closed wounds do not penetrate the entire thickness of the skin, so there is a bruise. The dog will be in pain and the wound will swell and feel hot to the touch. A cold compress relieves the pain. An open wound is more susceptible to infection than a closed. It must be bathed with an antiseptic, and cold water helps to stop the bleeding. Gauze and a bandage should be applied. Lacerated and puncture wounds should be seen by a vet.

6 TRAINING YOUR YORKIE

If you spoil your Yorkie – which is very easy due to his size and natural devotion to his owners – you must expect his demands on you to be great. A badly behaved Yorkie will become a nuisance rather than a pleasure, so it is important to instil some good manners in him.

Yorkies that are over-indulged usually belong to people who treat them as children rather than as dogs. As a result, the poor animal becomes totally confused by his position in the pack. This dog is the one who will end up in a rescue centre or be put to sleep due to his anti-social behaviour, such as being possessive over his food, toys and owner. I have met a few who were very bad, but who fortunately found homes with new families who understood their needs. True to character, the aggressive little tykes are now all good citizens. Their only wish in life is to be an agreeable friend.

Yorkies do not require the intensive training which some of the larger breeds need. Because they are so intelligent and willing to please their owners, they usually take to training quite quickly. Yorkies are such busy little dogs, they thrive on learning new things which keep their active minds occupied.

Any early training needs time and patience, or you will end up with a disobedient hooligan. For this reason, you should give plenty of time to your youngster – and, of course, the inevitable tender loving care. Do not assume your puppy will immediately fit himself into your expectations. Each command may take ten days to two weeks to penetrate, and, with some puppies, longer. Even after a lesson has been mastered, expect some confusion and a few slips.

Everything you do with the puppy must end on a good note. Reward him continually so he understands what you require. Never beat or threaten to beat him – either with your hand or a rolled-

The intelligent Yorkie can be trained to a high standard of Obedience.
Photo: Carol Ann Johnson.

up newspaper. To threaten him is as bad as hitting him and may make him hand-shy – where he will always cringe at an upraised hand. A rolled-up newspaper may not hurt the dog very much, but should never be used, because even the noise will scare him, and you should never train a dog by fear.

When you do correct him, make sure they are constructive corrections; they must show him instantly what he ought to be doing. For example, if, when training your Yorkie to sit, he does not understand what is required, then show him by guiding him into a sitting position with your hands.

Never consider training if you are in a bad mood – you will achieve nothing and undo any good your dog has already learnt; he will lose confidence in you and distrust you. Never work too long on any exercise or the puppy will become bored and, of course, he will tire quickly. Always reward him when he does a command correctly.

REWARD-BASED TRAINING

For any training, correction must be immediate, not ten seconds later. In training of any kind, correction is needed, not punishment. We must be confident in training, you in him and he in you. He must be confident that you are fair and trustworthy, and that a certain action will always be met with the same reaction. In training, this means that certain conduct is forbidden and other conduct is encouraged. Each action, when carried out correctly, can be rewarded with a treat. This will encourage him and he will surely learn quickly. Like corrections, rewards must also be given immediately so your Yorkie will understand when he has done something right.

If your dog is one that is not really interested in training and is easily distracted, use a squeaky toy or a treat to gain his attention. Do not give him the toy or treat until he has obeyed your command, then you can reward him and give lots of praise. While training your Yorkie, it is a good idea to use treats only at training times.

USING GOOD SENSE
Your Yorkie's senses can be utilised into making him easier to train.

SMELL: Your Yorkie's sense of smell is most important. His nose is extremely sensitive and linked to a well-developed sense of taste. Smelly treats – like cheese or liver – will help to get him motivated for training.

TASTE: Closely linked with his sense of smell. Most dogs, including many Yorkies, are ruled by their stomachs. Once he is rewarded with a treat, he is likely to try hard to earn another.

SIGHT: His eyes will tell you if he is enjoying his training or if he is plain bored. Your own attitude will determine your Yorkie's concentration. He will watch you and assess your actions, reading your body language. By being happy and positive, and smiling and talking to him, he should come on in leaps and bounds.

HEARING: A dog's hearing is far more acute than ours. Your Yorkie can hear frequencies of up to 70,000-100,000 vibrations per second, compared to our limit of 16,000 to 20,000. This is evident in him knowing when a familiar car is arriving, long before you are aware of it.

His sharp hearing means you do not have to shout commands. If the dog

Correction must be instantaneous – and so must reward.
Photo: Steve Nash.

does not respond to a command, it is not usually because he did not hear it, so it is no use repeating it at a higher volume. You do not want to end up shouting at your dog and making training an ordeal; it should be something you both enjoy. Be confident and use a firm, authoritative voice, together with lots of gentle encouragement to persuade your Yorkie to comply with your wishes.

TOUCH: Every dog loves to be touched by his owner. That gentle pat reassures him that all is well and you are friends. Reassurance is particularly important when training, as your Yorkie may be a little uncertain of what it is you require him to do. A quick pat or a cuddle when he gets something right will make sure he does not become too unsettled or nervous.

PUPPY TRAINING CLASSES

Puppy training classes can be fun. You will meet new people and your Yorkie will meet other dogs, so it can be very socialising for you both.

You will learn how to teach your pup the basic training commands (Sit, Down, Stay and Recall, and how to walk correctly on a lead) from someone who has had some experience with training dogs, young and old.

No trainer should be heavy-handed or shout at your puppy; if they do, find someone else who is of a more quiet disposition. So many trainers are used to large, strong dogs that need a really firm hand; so when you arrive with your Yorkie, some trainers can be perplexed. Despite being the smallest in the class, do not be surprised if your Yorkie outshines many of these larger dogs – Yorkies are fast learners!

The first classes can be harrowing. Since Yorkies are such tiny dogs, there is a danger that larger, boisterous puppies can intimidate your pup or accidentally hurt him. If it is a specialist puppy class that is supervised carefully, it is often worth letting the dogs sort themselves out. Keeping your pup away from larger pups may mean he grows up to fear them, so it is often worth letting your puppy interact with other pups of all shapes and sizes, so he grows up feeling equal to any dog he may meet in the park. Despite their size, Yorkies are more than capable of handling themselves. Be close by to make sure things do not get out of hand, and to remove your Yorkie if they do.

BASIC TRAINING

TEACHING "NO"

Your puppy should be taught the word "No". Use it to let him know when he is doing something you disapprove of, such as chewing your shoes or your furniture. When you use it, use a firm voice, and distract him from what he is doing. As soon as he stops, praise him and give him a treat.

SIT

This is a very useful command, which is easy to teach. You can start training from a very young age. Each time you see the pup going into a sit, say "Sit" and praise him. He will soon associate the action of sitting with the word. After a few repetitions you may be able to say "Sit" and he will obey. If you ask him to sit before giving him his food, he will learn that sitting on command is an enjoyable experience – as it is followed by a meal!

Some pups do not find it this easy, though, and will need a bit more encouragement by being shown exactly what is required of them. Put a collar and lead on your pup, hold the lead in the right hand, and, with the dog on your left, use your left hand to gently push down his hindquarters, giving the command "Sit!". If you gently pull the

*Gentle pressure applied on the hindquarters will ease the dog into the Sit.
Photo: Steve Nash.*

*Build up the Stay exercise gradually.
Photo: Steve Nash.*

lead up, it will stop him from lying down or squirming about. Repeat this a few times and he will quickly learn. As soon as he obeys, reward him with a tidbit.

DOWN

You can teach your puppy this command in a similar way to how you taught him to sit. Use the word "Down" when your Yorkie lies down naturally. Otherwise, kneel down in front of the pup; take a treat in your hand and, when the dog is standing, move your hand down to the ground between the dog's front paws. Do not allow the dog to take the treat until he lies down, then reward and praise him while he is in this position.

STAY

This command means your puppy should remain stationary wherever he is. When your pup will happily go into a Sit position, gradually build up the time before you release him. Praise him and repeat the commands "Sit" and "Stay".

For the first few times, do not try to

*Many dogs are more steady in the Stay when they are put into the Down position.
Photo: Steve Nash.*

make him stay more than 10-20 seconds before releasing him. Slowly increase the time until he will stay for a couple of minutes. As he progresses, you can take a step away from him, but keep the gentle praise going, to reassure him. It is important that you are close enough never to allow him to alter his position.

Each time he gets up before you release him, go back to practising for just short intervals at a time, with you standing closer to him.

When your Yorkie sits quietly for a

couple of minutes, you can practise the Stay in the Down position. Never forget to reward him verbally and with his tidbit.

RECALL

Your puppy has known his name for a few months and every time you have called him, he has come to you, so this will make this lesson easier. But what if you want him to come, and he is busy? You must train him to come whether he wants to or not.

The lesson to "Come" is a natural follow-up to the "Sit-stay". Begin the lesson by running through the previous two commands (Sit and Stay) as a warm-up. This will also give the pup the confidence in what he knows he can do. It can be helpful to enlist the help of a family member or a friend who can hold the pup, while you go a short distance away. Call the pup by name, followed by the word "Come". A sharp sound – like clapping your hands – will not only gain his attention, but make him come running to you, licking and grinning. To your pup's way of thinking, it is always fun to return to you, and he will learn quickly, especially if he is rewarded with a treat!

LEAD-TRAINING

As soon as your pup can go out, you can start lead-training. If your pup is of a happy disposition and used to following you in the house, there will be no problem. It is a good idea to put a collar on him for a couple of days in the house, so that he can get accustomed to the feel, prior to his debut into the big world.

Should your Yorkie fight and tug when you first take him out on his collar and lead, stoop down with the lead at arm's length and encourage him to come to you. Do this a few times and he will soon be trotting along beside you. Never let him pull in front. Check this early in training – it is a bad habit to develop.

THE SKY'S THE LIMIT

OBEDIENCE

Once you've mastered the basics with your puppy, there is nothing stopping you continuing training into the dog's adulthood. How far you both go is dependent on you and your dog's abilities. Only one Yorkie, to my knowledge, has competed at Crufts dog show. This was in 1973 and it was the first time a Toy dog had competed in the Obedience ring at Crufts. The Yorkie's name was Shandy, owned by Mrs Joyce Burton. He was placed fifth with a score of 295 out of a possible 300. Quite a feat for a Yorkie!

It is not at all unusual to see a little beribboned Yorkie in one of the Obedience rings in America. Many, many Yorkies complete their CD (Companion Dog) degree; many also go on to complete their CDX (Companion Dog Excellent) degree and a few even compete for the coveted title of UD (Utility Dog). The first AKC UD Yorkie in Utah is a dog named Sammy, owned by Deborah Nendell. Sammy is also the first dog in Utah to hold a multi-registry title – he also holds the title of ASCA CD which is the Companion Dog degree issued by the Australian Shepherd Club of America. This degree follows AKC rules, but they offer their own titles since the breed was slow to be accepted into AKC. Sammy also has 3 UDX legs which makes him a 'Superdog' and two legs toward his ASCA CDX title. Sammy is also a registered therapy dog and holds the Canine Good Citizen award.

If considering Obedience training, do consider your own Yorkie's aptitude. Any Obedience work requires heelwork, which is fine for a dog at knee-height, but, with a Yorkie, it becomes toe-work.

If your Yorkie has natural talent, enrol him at an Obedience training school. You will be taught by someone with a great deal of experience in this field. Remember that some trainers are better than others, so it is worthwhile finding a good one, preferably someone interested in taking you and your Yorkie on. You will be taught: heel work, sits, sit-stays, down-stays, retrieving, sniffing out scents, sendaways and distance control.

For this breed, the sendaway can be particularly difficult as most Yorkies are reluctant to leave their owners. This is especially the case if you are tense at competing, as this nervousness will be transmitted to your dog.

When you start to compete, you will be placed by a judge, who will score you on each exercise. Local training schools hold Obedience shows, which is a good place to start, as these are not so intense. You will progress from beginner to novice classes, to open Obedience classes. Provided your Yorkie has sufficient talent, you can then move on to working for that coveted Obedience Champion title.

OTCH Tattlers Take A Chance UDX is one of only two Yorkies to have gained the coveted title of Obedience Trials Champion. Bred and owned by Nancy Douce.
Photo: Pets by Paulette.

U-CH, UAG Brigshire TS Exis NA, NJC showing off agility skills.

GR-CH, UAG-1 Brigshire Rosemary Lace Exis NA, NAJ NJC clearing the hurdles. Tien Tran Photography.

MINI-AGILITY

Yorkshire Terriers, with their intelligence, dedication, speed and dexterity make excellent Agility dogs, and are real crowd-pleasers at the trials.

Agility is best described as a canine obstacle course, where dogs have to tackle various pieces of equipment with precision and speed. It is a reasonably new dog sport which began in 1978, when a group of enthusiasts put together the elements of working trials, Obedience and show-jumping. A demonstration event was put on at Crufts the same year, which was very well received by trainers and the general public. Since then, it has become incredibly popular, with owners of many different types of breeds.

Smaller dogs can compete in Mini-agility, where the jumps are not as high as for the standard course. Mini-agility is right up a Yorkie's street – the busy little dog can use himself well here, going through tunnels, and racing in and out of obstacles at full gallop. The dog is probably more suited than many of his owners – the handlers also have to be quite agile and fit!

Agility is rewarding for both the dog and its owner, requiring many loving and rewarding hours of training together. Many of the successful competitiors train on a daily basis. Most training clubs require a basic obedience course to be completed, as most of the work is done off leash, requiring handler control of the dog. Also the dog must be able to complete a sit- or down-stay on the table for the required count. Training methods vary from food, praise or toy motivation and may require a combination to be used.

During the late 80s and early 90s, Vanessa Levi had some success in the UK with her Trisdene Yorkies. Her Trisdene Temptation has been placed in numerous national Agility competitions. Vanessa's Yankee Doodly Dandy of Trisdene (Tristin), qualified for the Agility competition at Crufts in 1990 and 1991, and is one of the smallest UK dogs to compete in Mini-agility to date.

Agility is the fastest growing dog sport in the US with AKC licensed events growing from 377 in 1998 to 598 in 1999. The number of Yorkshire Terriers earning standard titles increased from 15 in 1998 to 27 in 1999.

Pam Wengorovius who lives in Belmont, Michigan, has enjoyed training and competing with her Yorkies in Agility Gr. Ch. Brigshire Rosemary Lace Exis NA, NAJ, NJC is one of her Yorkies with which she has been successful at Agility trials.

With their independent attitude, Yorkies always keep you on your toes, making both training and competing a rewarding and challenging experience.

FREESTYLE

Misha is the second Yorkie in Utah to receive a UD title in Obedience and she and her owner, Susan Colledge, also entertain doing Freestyle a series of Obedience movements set to music.

Susan and Misha do not compete in Freestyle competitions as these are mostly held on the East Coast and travel expenses can become prohibitive, but Susan and Misha gave a stirring performance at the YTCA National Specialty held in New Orleans, Louisiana, in October 1998. Misha took time off from her stage performance in *The Wizard of Oz,* where she played Toto, to appear in New Orleans with Susan.

Misha is also a Therapy Dog and makes one or two visits per week at nursing homes, schools, retirement homes, etc.
Misha and Susan have performed at the AKC Invitational three years in a row; Misha's picture appeared in *Sports Illustrated* and they have performed all over the country doing their Freestyle dance routine.

TRACKING

Arlene King of Hoffman Estates, Illinois, is the proud owner of Illusion's Sarah Ferguson ('Fergie') TD (Tracking Dog). Tracking is a sport where the dog is trained to follow the track that a person has laid and to find the article (usually a glove or a wallet) at the end of the track. Fergie started training

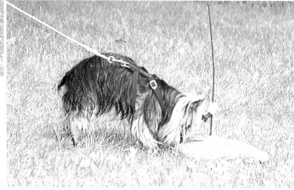

Illusion's Sarah Ferguson TD, CGC, TDI, owned by Arlene King. 'Fergie', in harness, working a track.

'Fergie' indicating the glove at the end of the track.

when she was just four months old and weighed only about 2¹/₂ lbs. She was so small that the only harness that would fit her was a bright pink fluorescent cat harness.

Her training was started with Arlene enlisting the aid of a friend to hold Fergie while Arlene laid a short track with a glove at the end that was filled with food. Then, Arlene would hide, and Fergie was told to "find it". Fergie very quickly figured out that, by using her nose, she not only was rewarded with a 'treat' but 'Mommie' would also appear with lots of praise, too. Tracking is taught using various motivational methods; this method of food and praise suited Fergie just fine.

As soon as the dog understands what it needs to do, the length of the track is increased, turns are added, and the track is 'aged' before the dog is started on it again. Ageing involves laying the track several hours prior the dog running it, thus allowing for other animal odours, wind and weather to play a part in

'ageing' the owner's scent.

Before a dog can enter an AKC Tracking Test it must be certified by a judge who will lay a regulation track and watch the dog run it; if the dog is successful, the judge will certify that the dog is ready for a test.

In October 1998 Fergie passed the very first test in which she was entered and became one of only a handful of Yorkies with a Tracking title. Fergie and Arlene are now working toward a TDX (Tracking Dog Excellent) title; this test is run in fields like the TD test but the track is longer, has more turns and crossturns, is aged at least three hours, and the dog needs to find multiple articles.

Variable Surface Tracking (VST) is totally different and the dog needs to learn to track on grass, concrete, asphalt, etc. This type of tracking is an urban version of the sport and is usually run in places like office complexes where the dog must track up and down stairs and around buildings. Yet, in a sport where a small dog is at a distinct disadvantage, Fergie has proven over and over that Yorkies have ability the accomplish anything they set their minds to.

TRAINING THE SHOW DOG

RING TRAINING

It is at ring training class that your young hopeful will socialise with other dogs. Once he has completed his course of inoculations and can walk on a collar and lead, you should contact your national kennel club for details of clubs in your area. Many dogs start at about four or five months of age. If this is the first time you are entering the world of show dogs, you will be meeting like-minded people – some beginners like yourself, but others with many years' experience with dogs. Learn from them, as they are an invaluable source of knowledge.

If your Yorkie is a little reluctant at ring classes, do not despair – some Yorkies need plenty of encouragement and confidence to move in a usually small hall with many strange dogs, of all shapes and sizes. I have owned many a show dog who has been reluctant to show off their potential at ring training classes. I took my Ch. Out Of The Blue for the first time at four months, accompanied by a friend who has shown Keeshonds for many years. My little Yorkie spent the evening enveloped in the Keeshond's coat, not wanting to leave him and hating every other dog in the hall. She never went again, her training taking place in the show ring. By the time she was two years old, she had got the message and managed to accumulate 23 CCs (you need three to become a Champion in the UK).

However, I do not advise the novice to take this course. It is worth persevering with ring training classes if you are a complete novice, as you will learn a lot about showing.

It is also here that your dog will learn how to stand on a table. All Yorkies are assessed as to their coat texture, colour and conformation on a table. Ring training will give your Yorkie experience of being handled by strangers which will stand him in good stead for being handled by judges in the future. The judge will check his mouth for the formation of his jaws and teeth, handling him for his conformation as set down in the Breed Standard and, of course, his quality and texture of coat. Many a dog can have all the attributes required, but can be beaten by a dog of slightly inferior quality, simply because he is handled so well, and shows off his attributes to such advantage that he outclasses his dour competitor. So it is down to you to get the best out of your future show Yorkie.

You will be shown how to walk your dog correctly. Many judges require you to walk in a triangle, and up and down. Some want the whole Yorkie class off their boxes to walk round the ring first. I dread these words, as a pup cannot

The show Yorkie must learn to walk on a loose lead. Photo: Steve Nash.

By tradition, the Yorkie is shown on a red box. Photo: Steve Nash.

wait to play with all these new playmates, and any training can go straight out the window! With a raw, high-spirited youngster, it is worth getting in towards the end, so that there are plenty of young pups like himself in front to occupy his mind, and not many pups behind him. This works well for me and my youngsters. With your concentration and handling, you can turn an inexperienced pup into appearing the opposite.

At this stage, you should be working with your pup as one, understanding his mind, reading every movement of his body. This has to work both ways: he should be receptive to a word spoken, a gentle touch and every move you make. Keep his attention and interest at all times, and this relationship will develop into adulthood, where literally a single look or slight touch will tell your dog

what you want of him – and he is only too willing to obey your every wish.

Training your vivacious Toy terrier to show off his assets in the ring is down to you, and your own character plays a role in how your dog is going to act in the show ring. If you are shy and an introvert, it will follow that your dog will be too. If you are an extrovert, your dog is likely to be confident and flashy, and will have a greater advantage over the introverted dog.

ON THE BOX
All Yorkies in the UK are shown on boxes with covers. This practice harks back to when the very early dog shows were held in public houses, which would have had sawdust on the floor. The long-coated silky terriers were shown on stools to prevent soiling the coat, and thus it has stayed.

7 GROOMING AND COAT CARE

There is so much to be learnt about grooming and presenting the Yorkie – but if the coat quality is not in his genetic make-up, no amount of brushing, oiling, conditioning, or any other home-made potions, will produce a good Yorkie coat.

A great amount of care is required to keep the coat in peak condition. Feeding, exercise and grooming go hand-in-hand. Correct feeding produces a healthy dog, and is reflected in a healthy coat, and with the right amount of exercise, your Yorkie will reach peak condition.

Your dog must be kept free from all parasites, so make sure you keep his worm and flea treatments up to date. It only takes one flea to make your Yorkie scratch, and hence ruin his coat. Flea infestation can also result in worms, which can also make the coat dull and lifeless.

TOOLS OF THE TRADE
Like anyone who has a job to do, you need the best tools available. Combs and pure bristle brushes are the best tools. Buy the brushes from antique shops. They should be good-quality with a fair length of bristle, and not too soft. A collection of these will not go amiss, since each coat texture requires a different brush.

The length of bristle on the brush is important. Long bristles are best, as the bristles can reach down through the coat to the skin. Nylon bristles are far too harsh for a Yorkie's luxurious coat; a natural bristle brush is best.

You will also need a comb, and a brush for oiling the coat, which should be kept apart from your best show brushes and combs. Your comb should have both wide and fine teeth to deal with different coat textures and different-sized knots.

The shampoo and conditioner you

Pure perfection in the Yorkshire Terrier's coat – Ch. Osmilion Signification, owned and bred by Osman Sameja.
Photo: Marc Henrie.

use will also determine the finish of his coat. Using harsh shampoos (e.g. strong, concentrated flea shampoo) can damage his tresses, too. There are so many shampoos and conditioners on the market that choosing which one to use can only be done by experimenting and seeing which one is best for your individual dog. When you find one that produces a good silky coat, it is probably best to stick with it.

I cannot overemphasise the importance of quality grooming equipment. The brushes you use will

Use top-quality natural, bristle brushes which will not damage the coat.
Photo: Steve Nash.

determine the final presentation of your show dog as the finished article. It is worth paying extra for a decent brush, as this is an investment for years.

If showing your Yorkie, you will also require a show box (to show him on, and for transportation), and a red or blue box cover, tissue paper, rubber bands, water spray, show lead, red or blue ribbon, scissors, and nail clippers. A good hair-dryer is essential, either a hand-held one, or a professional dryer on a stand. Don't try to economise on these purchases either. Much of this equipment can be bought from most Yorkshire Terrier clubs.

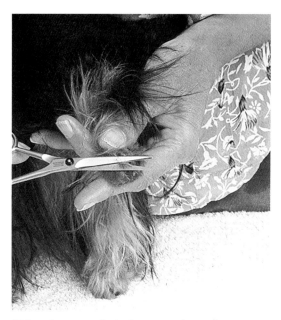

Trim the excess hair between the pads.

PRE-GROOM ROUTINE

FEET AND NAILS

Any excess hair between the dog's pads will need to be cut away and the foot trimmed neatly. Examine the pads to check there are no cuts. Check if his nails need cutting. If they do, cut the ends with guillotine clippers, being careful to avoid the quick of the nail.

TEETH

It is important to check his teeth regularly since Yorkies are prone to losing their teeth at a young age, so cleaning (and even descaling by your vet) will keep his teeth healthy for many years. Brush his teeth with a toothbrush or fingerbrush. Special meat-flavoured canine toothpaste will make it more of an enjoyable experience for your Yorkie.

Use guillotine nail-clippers to cut the nails.

EYES

Wipe the eyes with cotton wool (cotton) soaked in water, to remove any discharge. Dry the area with cotton wool.

EARS

Check his ears for ear mites or wax, and treat if necessary with proprietary drops or powder. A brown smelly discharge will indicate mites are present. If there is any unnecessary hair in the ear canal, pluck the hair out with tweezers, but first put in some ear powder and pluck only a few hairs at a time. The powder will help the hair come out easily and prevent the ear becoming sore.

ANAL GLANDS

Check his anus to make certain it is clean. If it is not, wash this area and dry it to prevent loss of hair. You may also need to empty the anal glands This job can be done in the bath prior to washing your Yorkie.

These are two small glands situated each side of the anus. The fluid they contain is yellowish-brown and very smelly. If the glands should become full, you can feel them more readily if you pass your fingers each side of the anus just below the tail.

By holding a piece of cotton wool (cotton) in one hand, the other hand can gently squeeze the glands and empty the pungent contents on to the

Thorough teeth-cleaning is required on a regular basis.

Check the ears for build-up of wax.

Before bathing, give the coat a brush through, checking for any mats or tangles.

Photo: Amanda Bulbeck.

cotton wool. If you are at all uncertain about this procedure, ask your vet to do them for you, where you can observe the procedure.

INITIAL BRUSH-THROUGH

Groom your Yorkie thoroughly down to the skin. Remove any knots and tangles, paying particular attention to the stomach, the inside back legs, and under the arms. Make sure you can comb the coat easily before putting your Yorkie in the bath. If you leave any knots or tangles, they will be made worse by rubbing the coat with shampoo, and you will be left with awful mats which will result in coat loss as you try to remove them.

Any large knots or mats will need to be cut out. Cut the mat right through the centre with a pointed pair of scissors, and work from the bottom of the knot outwards. The most common places for knots are under the elbows, behind the ears, and between the hind legs and belly.

BATHING

How often your Yorkshire Terrier is bathed depends on the environment and climate. Show dogs may need to bathed every week, though some pet dogs can be left for a month or more. Never bath a dog that appears unwell. If bathing a bitch in whelp, do so before she is heavy with pups.

Before you begin to bath your Yorkie, let him out to relieve himself, as it may be some time before he will have an opportunity again. You should keep him in for a while after grooming: if his coat is a little damp, you do not want him to catch a chill.

Bathing should be done efficiently and gently for your dog's comfort. Prepare everything needed for his bath beforehand. Run the water in the basin or bath, and get all the equipment needed so it is on hand:

Non-slip rubber mat
Shampoo
Conditioner
Towels
Hair-dryer
Cotton wool (cotton) for ear plugs
Clean brush and comb.

While you are bathing him, be sure to check any unusual lumps which may have appeared, especially if he is an older dog. Work briskly but gently, and talk to him throughout the process to reassure him. It is a good idea to keep one hand on him while bathing him, or he may leap out of the bath, with unfortunate results.

Some dogs do not like getting water in their ears. If your Yorkie objects, plug his ears with cotton wool (cotton), being careful not to push it too far into the ear.

The bath water should be lukewarm. Test it before using it on your dog. Wet his body thoroughly with either a spray or a jug. Leave the head for the moment – for once his head is wet, he will unquestionably shake himself.

Many shampoos are better if diluted, so carefully read the instructions on the shampoo and conditioner. Pour the shampoo on to the neck, shoulders, back, and rear end. Take care not to tangle his coat. Use your finger tips to massage the shampoo gently through his entire body and down his legs. Do not forget the stomach and underneath the tail.

Once the body has been well lathered and washed, you can wet your Yorkie's head. Apply the water to his head and face very carefully so as not to scare him. Once his head is thoroughly wet, apply the shampoo. I use a very mild shampoo on my dogs' heads, such as a baby shampoo. Work it into a lather, making sure to avoid the eyes. This can be achieved by covering the dog's eyes with the thumb and forefinger, at the same time tilting the head upwards, so that the water and lather will run backwards away from the eyes. Rinse well with the spray or jug, protecting his eyes once more.

It may be necessary to shampoo him again, depending how dirty he is. If so, repeat the procedure, rinsing thoroughly at the end.

Add conditioner, and work through the coat with your fingers. Many conditioners are meant to be left on for a short period of time. Rinse through a couple of times with clean water.

BATHING
Photos: Amanda Bulbeck.

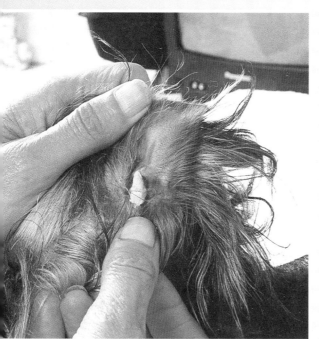
1. Insert ear-plugs before bathing.

2. Wet the coat, ensuring the water is lukewarm.

3. Make sure the coat is thoroughly soaked.

4. Take special care wetting the head.

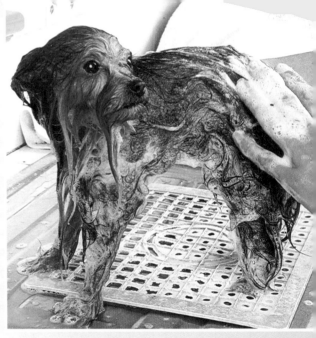

5. *Some Yorkies will tolerate a shower spray.*

6. *Use your finger tips to massage in the shampoo.*

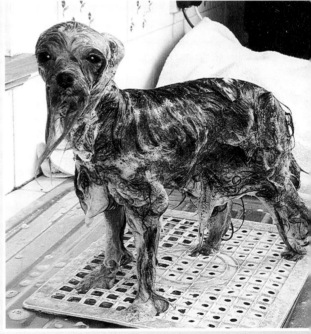

7. *Use a mild shampoo for the head.*

8. *The shampoo is worked into every part of the coat.*

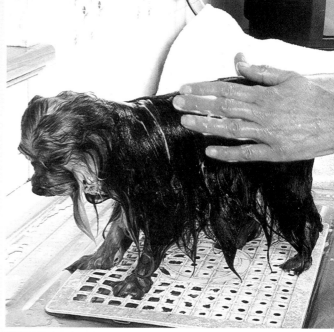

9. Apply conditioner.

10. Massage the conditioner into the coat, and then rinse the coat thoroughly.

DRYING

There are many dryers on the market. The type you buy will entirely depend on how often you use it. If it is only for occasional use, a human hair-dryer is more than adequate. If you have several Yorkies and attend regular shows, it may be worth investing in a professional grooming dryer on a stand. Although this type is more costly, it has the advantage of holding the dryer for you, so you have both hands free to handle and groom your dog.

I find it best to work on a table, bringing the dog up to waist height. Dry your dog's head with a towel before moving on to the other parts of the body. At this stage, your Yorkie will probably have a very good shake. Cover him in the towel and squeeze out the excess moisture before rubbing very gently – do not be vigorous, or you will create huge knots! Do not forget to remove the ear plugs.

Lay him on a thick dry towel to dry him, starting with the head. Make sure the dryer is not too hot for him – keep checking throughout the session. Brush the coat gently, lifting it, rather than flattening it. Dry from the roots, and brush as you dry, which will help to straighten the coat.

When his head is dry, start drying the rest of his coat, using the same method. Do not stop until the coat is bone-dry.

If it is a very hot day, and your dog is panting, dry him with the dryer set to

1. It is important not to rub vigorously when using a towel. Wrap the dog in the towel and gently squeeze to remove excess moisture.

2. A professional grooming dryer enables you to have both hands free so that you can brush while you dry.

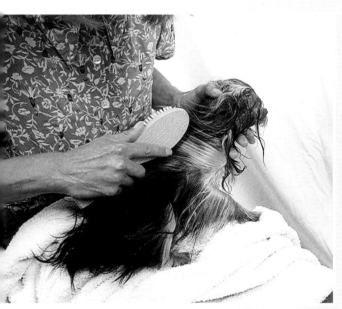

3. Lift the coat up when brushing it rather than flattening it.

4. Make sure the air from the dryer is not too hot, and direct it so that you are drying from the roots.

5. *Take special care with the head.*

6. *Continue brushing until the coat is completely dry.*

the 'cool' setting, if your dryer has this function.

GROOMING

Your Yorkie should be groomed carefully every day. Not only does this help to keep knots at bay, but the act of brushing massages the skin and encourages good blood circulation. If left for a couple of weeks, you will end up with a horrendous chore on your hands, trying to disentangle the long matted coat. This will be very time-consuming, and will be painful to your dog. You will also destroy a great deal of his coat, resulting in several months' work to repair the damage.

Do not let it get this far. Grooming your Yorkie can be great fun, and it can be relaxing therapy, provided you do it regularly. A daily groom will take a fraction of the time compared to an hour-long session if your Yorkie develops knots. Never look on grooming as a dreary chore – it should be an enjoyable bonding session for you both.

Make sure your dog gets used to the routine of grooming. It should be at the same time every day, with the same sequence of procedures so the dog always knows that to expect next.

Never stop his grooming because he is being difficult, as this will reward his bad behaviour. Instead, go over an area that he likes, and talk to him in a reassuring way. When he has calmed

BRUSHING

Photos: Amanda Bulbeck.

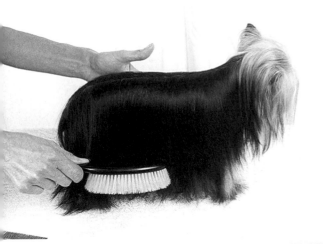

1. *A parting must be made from behind the ears to the tip of the tail.*

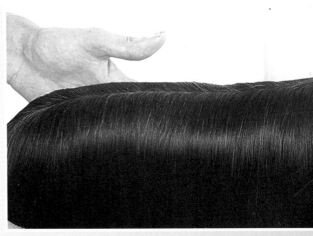

2. *The parting must be absolutely straight so that the coat falls naturally.*

3. *Be gentle when brushing around the face.*

4. *A comb can be used for the 'beard'.*

down, gradually move on to grooming other areas of his body. Never fight or bully him, as he will always associate grooming with a bad experience. A treat at the end of each grooming session will encourage him to believe that grooming is pleasurable and should not be feared.

FINAL PARTING

Make a parting from behind the ears to the tip of his tail, with a comb, and brush the hair to each side. Start brushing his head, moustaches and falls (the golden hair on the cheeks up to the base of the ear). Be very gentle around the face, so as not to poke him in the

TYING THE TOP-KNOT
Photos: Amanda Bulbeck.

1. Comb the head hair forwards.

2. Smooth it backwards and secure with an elastic band.

3. It is important that the top-knot is not secured too tightly as it must be comfortable for the dog.

4. Traditionally a red ribbon is used in the show ring.

5. When the bow is tied, it can be trimmed with scissors.

eyes with the bristles. Brush carefully on either side of the eyes. Pass down the neck and over his body, brushing each side of his body from the parting down. Brush the tail and each leg in turn. Finish off by brushing his belly, and give him a big kiss and lots of fuss to reward him.

Once your Yorkie is lovely and clean, do make sure that his bedding and sleeping quarters are as clean as he is.

GROOMING FOR THE SHOW RING

There can be many disappointments in breeding the show dog, but coat quality and colour are of the utmost importance. The hard work for you now begins. For the whole of your dog's show career his coat must be crackered regularly, oiled, bathed and generally kept as a precious jewel. A firm bond will develop between you and your dog, which I find one never quite gets with a pet dog, probably due to the intensity of the show dog's care.

Neglect the show Yorkie for just a short period of time and you will spend weeks trying to repair the damage, and getting him back to full show condition.

When in the show ring, observe the other dogs. If another dog has a more luxurious coat than your dog's, do not be afraid to ask the owner for any tips or advice.

BATHING AND DRYING
The safest place to do this is in the bath with a spray. As I have already described bathing, I will only add here how important the drying is. Dry from the roots with a good blow dryer, brushing as you dry. This helps to straighten the coat. Be very gentle with the head. When your dog is completely dry, trim his ears if necessary and tie up his head and body in clean crackers.

Yorkies that are shown frequently will require a bath the day before, or on the morning of, the show (depending on the time of the class and the distance you have to travel). Yorkies quickly get used to any routine, and if a bath is part of your dog's weekly routine, he will quickly accept it and even enjoy it, along with the grooming and paraphernalia that it entails. Wash and dry him as described earlier

When his coat is completely dry, you can apply oil to it, by simply dipping the oiling brush in oil lightly and working through your Yorkie's coat by brushing. I have found nothing better than almond oil for silky coats. You will then tie up his head and body in clean crackers.

CRACKERING/WRAPPING
Invariably, a show dog is put into crackers. Crackering, or wrapping, involves tying up the dog's coat to cultivate its wealth and grow it to great lengths, especially the beard and moustaches. Basically, crackering keeps

1. Dip the brush in a shallow dish of oil.

2. Brush the oil through the coat.

3. Work from the root of the hair, brushing upwards.

4. Work with care when you brush through the head hair.

the dog clean and free of tangles and knots and makes it easier for the owner to cope with a luxurious coat, although it does involve plenty of brush power from the owner!

Take a piece of acid-free tissue paper approximately A4 in size, fold the bottom about a quarter of the way up,

and then fold it in half lengthways. The cracker is made and ready to receive the hair.

Crackering can be done as soon as the coat starts to become tangled and generally looks untidy. Start crackering too young and you will pull out the coat, ending up with a thin, straggly coat as a junior. Some textures never recover from this early intervention, while others grow and grow no matter what you do to them, and are only enhanced by crackering.

Some show kennels only tie up the hair on their dogs' heads, leaving the body coat to grow naturally. This, of course, involves a great deal of work to keep the coat clean and tangle-free.

A STEP-BY-STEP GUIDE

The first cracker to be put in your dog will be the top-knot. This is usually a haphazard affair at first but, once it's in and the youngster hasn't ripped it out, you have achieved your first goal. I usually get someone to hold the dog steady when first attempting the top-knot.

Take a line from the corner of the eye to the base of the ear on each side of the head. Gathering the hair together from the back, take a straight line from the base of the ear across to the other. Now lay the top-knot in the centre of the cracker paper and fold the paper over to the left and then to the right, securing the hair. Fold the paper in half and then in half again and secure it with a rubber band. Make sure that nothing is pulling to cause discomfort to the dog – if it is, the dog will promptly rip it out! Make it as neat as possible.

When the youngster has got used to his new hair-do and readily accepts the top-knot cracker, you can progress to tying up his moustaches, provided there is enough hair to tie up. Generally speaking, take a line from the inside of the eye to the edge of the lip of the mouth. I find that the actual line from the eye depends on the dog's head and length of muzzle. At this stage, the whiskers are meagre, so a small cracker is all that's needed. A cracker under the chin also can be put in at this stage.

When crackering the moustaches, take care not to tie up any of the hair from under the chin at the same time, as this would cause great discomfort and prevent the dog from eating. Always check when you have crackered your dog's head that he can open his mouth.

After a couple of weeks, the falls can be put up.

As the dog matures, the body coat will be tied up. Having finished the head, just follow down the blue coat, the neck, shoulder, rib, loin and rump, finishing off with the tail. This makes five crackers down each side of the parting. Keep them neat and tidy and the coat well oiled. In the course of this, the oil attracts dirt and dust, so the dog must be bathed regularly, re-oiled and crackered up.

After crackering always let the dog have a good shake and stretch.

Boots can be kept on your dog's hind legs if he is inclined to scratch, as this will prevent loss of coat on his head. I use the finger tube-gauze for this purpose.

CRACKERING

Photos: Amanda Bulbeck.

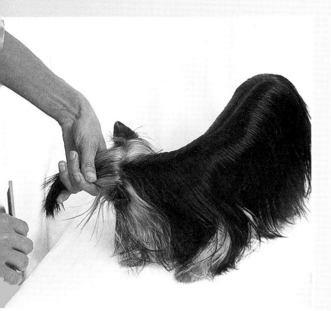

1. Comb the top-knot forward.

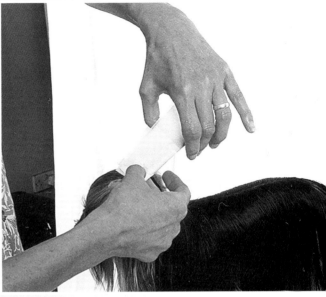

2. Lay the hair in the centre of the tissue paper and fold to the left , and then to the right.

3. Fold the paper in half.

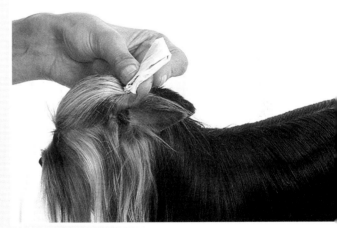

4. Fold it in half again.

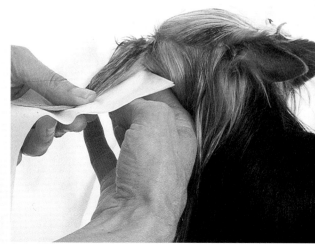

5. Secure with an elastic band.

6. Take a line from the inside of the eye to the edge of the lip when crackering the moustaches.

7. Repeat the process as for the top-knot, ensuring you do not catch up any hair from under the chin.

8. Fold the tissue paper.

CRACKERING

Photos: Amanda Bulbeck.

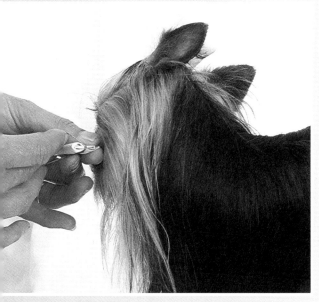

9. *Secure with an elastic band.*

10. *The head hair is now fully protected with crackers.*

11. *Follow the line of the body with crackers, finishing with the tail.*

PUTTING ON BOOTS
Photos: Amanda Bulbeck.

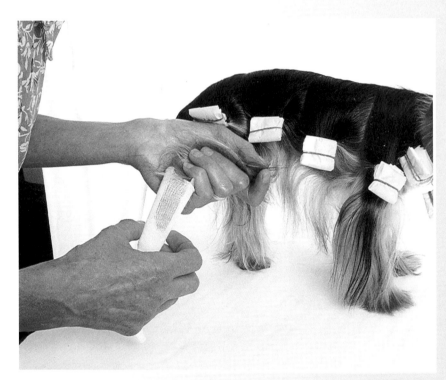

1. Gauze-tube boots can be put on the hindlegs to prevent scratching and damage to the head hair.

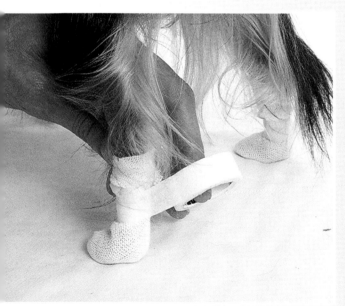

2. The boots are taped in position.

3. The boots perfectly comfortable – and the dog scarcely knows he is wearing them.

All the hard work pays off when you end up with your Yorkshire Terrier looking like this.

TRIMMING

There will come a time after all this work of cultivating the coat that it is now too long! It must be trimmed back to a reasonable length to prevent it impeding the Yorkie's movement in the show ring. After bathing and grooming the dog, stand him on the edge of the table, trim the coat to floor length or a little longer, depending on your preference. Trim the tan hair on the legs to the same length. Keep the hair on the feet trimmed at all times.

To trim the ears, you will need a good sharp pair of scissors. Cut around the dog's ear shape, going a third- to half-way down the ear. How good a job you do will depend on the dog's ear size and shape. A big bat-eared Yorkie will only have his ugly ears accentuated; a correct small ear can only be enhanced. After this, cut the hair on the back of the ear down about half-way, and cut it very short. Take the dog's head in your hands and see the effect. All Yorkies' heads vary, so tailor the trimming to enhance his head, not to detract from any other quality he has.

8 THE BREED STANDARDS

An official Breed Standard is required to assist judges and breeders to recognise the essential characteristics of the breed.

Before a written Breed Standard was produced, the Yorkshire Terrier was bred according to the ideal type described by word of mouth. The Yorkie was originally a ratter, but he evolved into the glamorous little dog we have today. Few 4-lb Yorkies can take on and kill an adult rat, but his original traits and characteristics would have allowed for his ability to kill vermin, as would his body structure. A tiny dog with a glorious coat – so new looking – would have quickly become an asset to a Victorian home as an expensive status symbol; and his ratting days would have become a somewhat distant memory.

By the 1870s, a Standard was being set down for breeders and judges to observe and be guided by. In *Dogs: Their Points, Whims, Instincts and Peculiarities*, edited by Henry Webb and published in 1872, we find this description of the Yorkshire Terrier:

The head rather long, with hair falling down considerably below the jaw, golden colour at the sides and on ears, also on the muzzle and moustaches; hair on the back long and perfectly straight, good rich blue and very bright; legs and feet well tanned and not too much feathered; tail perfectly straight and well carried; shape firm and compact, not too long on the legs, broad chest and tanned. The blue and tan should contrast so well as to please the eyes, rich and decided in colour, and not a sickly silver colour all over.

Apart from the head being 'rather long', the description is still applicable to the Yorkie today.

By 1883, a basic Standard was recognised, for the purposes of judging the breed; descriptions of the breed were printed in show catalogues and

Osman Sameja's Ch. Osmilion Dedication: The UK's top winning Yorkshire Terrier of all time.

articles. With the formation of the Yorkshire Terrier Club in 1898, an official Standard was approved. The club also drew up a Standard of points for judging:

Reading the Standard should conjure up a picture of the ideal Yorkshire Terrier – his body construction, head

Formation and terrier appearance	15
Colour of hair on body	15
Richness of tan on head and legs	15
Quality of texture of coat	10
Quantity and length of coat	10
Head	10
Mouth	5
Legs and feet	5
Ears	5
Eyes	5
Tail carriage	5
TOTAL	100

and coat colour, and coat texture. A Yorkie is a terrier in a glorious-coloured coat of great length and pure silk. This attribute is what has attracted so many people to the breed. Also remember that monetary gain would have played a part in his further development. This dog would have been so different from any other breed of its time; with his character, size and coat, there was no other dog quite like the Yorkie, especially with such a loving temperament. This would have resulted in fine specimens commanding high prices, and this has persisted well into this century where a good specimen is valued very highly.

The Kennel Club revised the old Breed Standard in 1950 so that judges and breeders could understand it more clearly. However, it was still open to being misinterpreted by judges and fanciers, so, in 1987, the Kennel Club (with the assistance of the Yorkshire Terrier clubs) revised the Standard once more, and the information was presented in a more logical and consistent sequence.

The Kennel Club, the American Kennel Club, and the Federation Cynologique Internationale (FCI) versions of the Standard vary very little, only a few words being different. The FCI judges Yorkies to the UK Standard. The US accepted the UK Standard in 1912, revising the Standard in 1966 for the very same reasons as the Kennel Club did in 1987.

Ch. Verolian Temptress With Ozmilion: Winner of 39 CCs – top winning bitch in the UK.

Both the AKC and the KC Standards are produced below, and I also give my own detailed interpretation of the Standards.

THE BRITISH STANDARD

GENERAL APPEARANCE: Long-coated, coat hanging quite straight and evenly down each side, a parting extending from nose to end of tail. Very compact and neat, carriage very upright conveying an important air. General outline conveying impression of vigorous and well-proportioned body.

CHARACTERISTICS: Alert, intelligent toy terrier.

TEMPERAMENT: Spirited, with even disposition.

HEAD AND SKULL: Rather small and flat, not too prominent or round in skull, nor too long in muzzle; black nose.

EYES: Medium, dark, sparkling, with sharp intelligent expression and placed to look directly forward. Not prominent. Edge of eyelids dark.

EARS: Small, V-shaped, carried erect, not too far apart, covered with short hair, colour very deep, rich tan.

MOUTH: Perfect, regular and complete scissor bite, i.e. upper teeth closely overlapping lower teeth and set square to the jaws. Teeth well placed with even jaws.

NECK: Good reach.

FOREQUARTERS: Well laid shoulders, legs straight, well covered with hair of rich golden tan a few shades lighter at ends than at roots, not extending higher on forelegs than elbow.

BODY: Compact with moderate spring of rib, good loin. Level back.

HINDQUARTERS: Legs quite straight when viewed from behind, moderate turn of stifle. Well covered with hair of rich golden tan a few shades lighter at ends than at roots, not extending higher on hindlegs than stifles.

FEET: Round; nails black.

TAIL: Customarily docked to medium length with plenty of hair, darker blue in colour than rest of body, especially at the end of tail. Carried a little higher than level of back.

GAIT/MOVEMENT: Free, with drive; straight action front and behind, retaining level topline.

COAT: Hair on body moderately long, perfectly straight (not wavy), glossy; fine silky texture, not woolly. Fall on head long, rich golden tan, deeper in colour at sides of head, about ear roots and on muzzle where it should be very long. Tan on head not to extend on to neck, nor must any sooty or dark hair intermingle with any of tan.

COLOUR: Dark steel blue (not silver blue), extending from occiput to root of tail, never mingled with fawn, bronze or dark hairs. Hair on chest rich, bright tan. All tan hair darker at the roots than in middle, shading to still lighter at tips.

SIZE: Weight up to 3.1 kg (7 lb).

FAULTS: Any departure from the foregoing points should be considered a fault and the seriousness with which the fault should be regarded should be in exact proportion to its degree.

NOTE: Male animals should have two apparently normal testicles fully descended into the scrotum.
Reproduced by kind permission of The Kennel Club.

THE AMERICAN STANDARD

GENERAL APPEARANCE: That of a long-haired toy terrier whose blue and tan coat is parted on the face and from the base of the skull to the end of the tail and hangs evenly and quite straight down each side of body. The body is neat, compact and well proportioned. The dog's high head carriage and confident manner should give the appearance of vigor and self-importance.

HEAD: Small and rather flat on top, the skull not too prominent or round, the muzzle not too long, with the bite neither undershot nor overshot and teeth sound. Either scissors bite or level bite is acceptable. The nose is black. Eyes are medium in size and not too prominent; dark in color and sparkling with a sharp, intelligent expression. Eye rims are dark. Ears are small, V-shaped, carried erect and set not too far apart.

BODY: Well proportioned and very compact. The back is rather short, the back line level, with height at shoulder the same as at the rump.

LEGS AND FEET: Forelegs should be straight, elbows neither in nor out. Hind legs straight when viewed from behind, but stifles are moderately bent when viewed from the sides. Feet are round with black toenails. Dewclaws, if any, are generally

BIS/BISS Am. Ch. Stratford Blue Max: A top winning Yorkie in the USA.

removed from the hindlegs. Dewclaws on the forelegs may be removed.

TAIL: Docked to a medium length and carried slightly higher than the level of the back.

COAT: Quality, texture and quantity of coat are of prime importance. Hair is glossy, fine and silky in texture. Coat on the body is moderately long and perfectly straight (not wavy). It may be trimmed to floor length to give ease of movement and a neater appearance, if desired. The fall on the head is long, tied with one bow in center of head or parted in the middle and tied with two bows. Hair on muzzle is very long. Hair should be trimmed short on tips of ears and may be trimmed on feet to give them a neat appearance.

COLOURS: Puppies are born black and tan and are normally darker in body color, showing an intermingling of black hair in the tan until they are matured. Color of hair on body and richness of tan on head and legs are of prime importance in adult dogs, to which the following color requirements apply:
Blue: Is a dark steel-blue, not a silver-blue and not mingled with fawn, bronzy or black hairs.
Tan: All tan hair is darker at the roots than in the middle, shading to still lighter tan at the tips. There should be no sooty or black hair intermingled with any of the tan.
Color on Body: The blue extends over the body from back of neck to root of tail. Hair on tail is a darker blue, especially at end of tail.
Headfall: A rich golden tan, deeper in color at sides of head, at ear roots and on the muzzle, with ears a deep rich tan. Tan color should not extend down on back of neck.

Chest and legs: A bright, rich tan, not extending above the elbow on the forelegs nor above the stifle on the hind legs.

WEIGHT: Must not exceed seven pounds.

Reproduced by kind permission of the American Kennel Club.

ANALYSIS OF THE STANDARDS

GENERAL APPEARANCE
A fine-boned, active toy terrier. Although small and fine, the Yorkshire Terrier should be solid in stature, and neither too long nor too low. His coat should be gleaming and hanging quite straight, with a parting from head to root of the tail, only interrupted by the topknot. There must be no coarseness, as the Yorkie carries himself proudly with head held high, giving an elegant appearance. I like to think of Yorkshire Terriers as models in evening gowns.

CHARACTERISTICS AND TEMPERAMENT
Always willing to learn, easy to train, quite fearless and very adaptable, the Yorkshire Terrier is the ideal pet. As a show dog, his sharpness and acumen, together with his lively talent of attracting everyone's attention, will make him stand out in the ring. Watching some Yorkie show dogs in the ring, their alertness and vivacious attitude can only be put down to their early ratter instincts.

HEAD AND SKULL

Rather small and flat, neither apple-shaped, like the Chihuahua, nor without a stop, like some other terriers. When viewed from the side, the muzzle should be half the length of the skull, and straight, not down-faced. Viewed from the front, no snipiness (pointedness) but a reasonably broad muzzle. The nose should be black. If there is lack of pigment on the nose (brown or pink), it usually follows that the edge of the eyelids will be pale or lacking in colour.

EYES

The eyes should be dark, framed with black eyelids, intelligent and very alert at all times; they should not be as almond-shaped as in the Poodle and not prominent as in the Pekingese or Chihuahua.

The AKC Standard groups the eyes, ears and mouth under 'Head'. When describing the eyes, it has omitted "placed to look directly forward". If the eyes are not placed like this, the entire expression of the dog is altered, and he stops looking so alert and terrier-like.

EARS

The ears are pricked, small, V-shaped and placed high on the head; they will indicate the dog's mood. Generally the hair on the back of the ear is stripped half-way down to show the true shape, and the hair is always a darker tan on the back of the ear than on the rest of the dog.

All Standards say the ears should not be "too far apart", but how far is too far? It is open to interpretation. As a guide, I suggest the ears frame the head and should balance it.

Being V-shaped, and not at all rounded, the ears give the Yorkie that perky prettiness. Large 'bat ears' are very unsightly and usually sit at 'ten to two'. Semi-erect or flop ears, although acceptable in early Breed Standards, are no longer permitted, and have no place in the show ring.

MOUTH

A bad mouth (undershot or overshot), although acceptable in a pet, is not correct for a show dog. The Breed

Typical head, with dark eyes, and bright alert expression.

Standard does not mention that the Yorkie should have 42 teeth: 20 in the upper jaw and 22 in the lower, the upper jaw consisting of 6 incisors (the biting teeth), 2 canines (for ripping and tearing), 8 premolars and 4 molars (the cutters and crushers), and the lower jaw having the same plus two extra molars.

Too few incisors can make the muzzle snipy, so a full mouth should be bred for. Years ago, one or two teeth missing was not considered too serious a fault, and some breeders – including myself – agree. The head shape, expression, and the small ears are far more important, as long as the jaw is level.

The FCI countries impose stricter

rulings when judging the teeth: a scissor bite is best, a pincer bite is still allowed, no incisor teeth should be missing, and only four premolars at most should be missing.

NECK AND BODY

The AKC Standard makes no mention of the Yorkie neck. The KC Standard simply states that the dog should have "good reach". The ideal neck should be muscular, moderately short, with no coarseness. As a ratter, the Yorkie would have required this type of neck to be able to grab, shake, and kill his quarry.

An overweight dog will lose his neck into his shoulders, making him appear dumpy. A long, thin neck would result in neck problems if the Yorkie was still involved in rat-catching, and such a neck will negate the dog's natural elegance.

The neck slopes gradually from a head carried high, joining the withers, shoulders and ribs in a streamlined fashion with no break in the contour. This is the perfect shoulder. The basis of a good shoulder lies mainly in the position of the scapula (shoulder bone) in relation to the dorsal vertebrae over which it lies.

It is influenced also by the height of the scapular spine, the length of the scapula and the length of the upper foreleg. On either side of the shoulder bone there is a hollow which contains muscle. If this is shallow, due to the lowness of the scapular spine, the

*Correct head proportions,
viewed in profile.*

contained muscle is likely to bulge outwards, giving rise to an overloaded shoulder.

A line drawn down the spine of the scapula, starting at the withers and ending at the shoulder joint, should form an angle of 90° with the humerus. In a straight shoulder the angle will be greater than 90°, making the shoulder appear more upright and affecting the dog's movement at the front.

The forelegs should be quite straight when standing and moving. There should be no plaiting (crossing one leg in front of the other) or daisy-cutting (not lifting the feet up enough), and the elbows should be close to the chest. The well-sprung ribs and chest should have plenty of heart and lung room (and not be slab-sided, with flattened ribs), giving a narrow appearance. The loin should be short and well muscled. Taken all together, good shoulders, well-formed ribs and good loin cannot fail to produce a level topline.

The hindquarters should have good width across the pelvic area, well-muscled upper thighs, a moderate bend of stifle and well-angulated hocks. The legs, viewed from the rear, should be quite straight, and when the dog is moving they should drive with power.

All Breed Standards agree on the shape of the Yorkshire Terrier and all read similarly (although, interestingly, the lay of the shoulders is not mentioned in the AKC Standard). However, they are still open to different interpretations, despite the revisions.

The Yorkie should appear square, but it is not the leg height which gives him this shape, it is a short loin (the region from the back rib to the pelvic bones). This muscular loin will give him the ability to manoeuvre quickly and move with great drive. A dog with a long weak loin will certainly not have this ability, and usually a weak loin accompanies a bad topline and poor hindquarters, and so the dog will not have the balance of his better-made counterparts.

Ch. Verolian Out Of The Blue, owned and bred by Veronica Sameja-Hilliard. Photo: Carol Ann Johnson.

Ch. Phalbrienz Floribunda: The only undocked Champion currently being shown in the UK.

The UK and FCI Standards mention that the tan hair on the forelegs should not extend higher than the elbow, and on the hindlegs should not extend higher than the stifles. The colour should be darker at the roots. This information is in the AKC Standard under the discussion on colour.

FEET
Round (not hare) feet, well-padded and with black nails kept short. Preferably, dewclaws should be removed.

TAIL
The tail is one of the most important parts of any Yorkie. You know by looking at the tail whether he is happy or sad, apprehensive or intimidated. I always think the ears and tail work together in this respect.

From *The Illustrated Book of the Dog* by Vero Shaw, published in 1881, we are told that the tail should be "cut and carried straight". But was this when standing or only when moving?

Many early pictures of Yorkies showed the tail tucked in with the line of the body giving a round-rump appearance. All the photos of Huddersfield Ben show him with his tail carried level, but his tail set is below the line of his back – and bear in mind that in all the photographs, he had paid a visit to the taxidermist!

I believe neither type of tail is wrong, since a gay-tailed dog can be outstanding. It is a matter of personal taste. My own opinion is that the tail should be concealed in his general outline when he is standing, not over his back like a teapot handle, or carried higher than the level of his back. I believe the Yorkie's tail should only be apparent when he moves, or when he wags it.

If docked, it is done to the tip of the tan marking.

GAIT
When moving, the Yorkie should give the impression of a very vigorous, happy Toy terrier, moving straight, fore and aft, with drive, and retaining a level topline at all times. The dog should cover plenty of ground as he moves.

COAT
The crowning glory of any mature

The characteristic vigorous happy gait of a Yorkie in full flow.

Yorkie is his coat – a wealth of metallic blue against rich golden tan. The adult dog's coat will gleam in the sun, reflecting the light, and consequently feeling cool to the touch. A black, woolly coat will not shine as much, nor will it feel cool, as it will absorb light and heat. The quality of the silken coat often depends on breeding.

Coat colour and texture will always be a radical topic in the breed. The AKC Standard places considerable emphasis on the coat texture and colour, and even includes details of the coat colour of a puppy's coat.

All three Standards agree on the type of coat: silky and blue with a rich tan on the head and legs. Colour is of great importance. The adult Yorkie usually reaches full colour by three years of age. During this process, its colour goes

through many transitions: from the black-and-tan pup, through the blue-headed infant and the 'badger-striped' adolescent, finishing up with the steel-blue-and-tan adult.

'Dark steel blue' covers quite a range of colour, from light to really dark blue. The depth of blue to the eye should be 'gun metal', again with that metallic finish. The word 'even' is not included in the Breed Standards, but the blue must be uniform throughout, with no patches or mingling tan hairs on the shoulders or hind legs.

Lighter blue and pale tan coloured Yorkies always seem to have an abundance of silken coat, and quite often waves too. A dark, woolly dog always remains dark and sooty-looking, and a solid, heavy tan seems to accompany the black coat, which will never break to a metallic blue. Many break to a slate colour, but they will feel cottony or woolly to the touch.

The coarse-coated dog is usually a solid tan, which is almost ginger (tan with no shading). These dogs have no hope in the show ring. This coat will never grow into a luxurious silk, and will just break off at the tips due to its brittleness, as the dog matures.

The Yorkie's neat head is framed with rich, golden tan moustaches and falls of great length, being darker on the muzzle, the side of the head and ears. Using the word 'rich' in relation to the tan colouring implies that it should be truly golden, not pale or washed out, and the word 'golden', that it should be like a polished gold coin, again with that metallic finish, able to reflect light. The tan should be darker at the roots than in the middle, and lighter at the tips. Only the correct silken texture can produce this requirement, and, in a quality coat, it is very evident on the legs.

'Glossy, fine silky texture' – the true texture, as I have said, is cool to the touch, and this hair is very strong and can grow to great lengths and shine

brilliantly, especially in the sunlight.

Some Yorkshire Terriers have a coat texture that is silky to the touch, and that even looks silky from the ring-side. Perhaps this is due to the conditioner used, but the colour never rings true. The blue body coat can shine and even feel silky, but I have found that it is in the tan that the true texture is found, and this type of Yorkie will grow a coat of length, but the head will not properly clear, so he always bears the black marks up the front of his head (from the stop to the top knot) and at the sides. As I have already stated, the coat quality comes from his breeding.

From the very early days, going as far back as 1881, the Yorkshire Terrier on the bench has been 'faked' – that is, his colour is altered to put him at an advantage over others in the ring. To show this, I again quote from *The Illustrated Book of the Dog* by Vero Shaw (1881):

There are unfortunately many unfair advantages by which a cunning and unprincipled person can steal a march on youth or inexperience. The beautiful colour of the body is the most usual mark for the skill of the faker. A common application is black-lead to the darker portion of the coat on the back.

We can assume that 'faking' has persisted well into this century.

Anyone who ever contemplates this has no care for the future of the breed and if the only reason for their actions is

The rich golden tan – a colour that should never appear pale or washed out.

The crowning glory – Ch. Ozmilion Mystification winning Best in Show, Crufts 1997.

to win top awards, they certainly have no care for the breed at all and should take up some other pursuit. The Yorkie is so unique in his distinctive coat and colouring, which puts him apart from any other breed of dog, that to tamper with his natural colour and thereby fool people into his genetic make-up, is criminal.

SIZE
Up to 3.1 kg (7lb). Dogs in the ring today do conform to this weight limit. Larger specimens can be very impressive but, at the end of the day, it has to be the overall dog and type rather than size that win. The larger dog must fit the Breed Standard and there must be no coarseness.

9 THE SHOW RING

Showing can be a very sociable event, opening up a whole new world for you, and allowing you to meet new people and make new friends. As in any competitive sport or hobby, you will also meet some horrid people, too; fortunately, these types do not stay in the breed for long! If you are determined to make each show a fun day, irrespective of the results, you will enjoy showing and make some lasting friendships.

The delight of presenting your dog from that raw puppy to the mature adult, the finished article in all his glory, is very rewarding. Showing means you are involved in the future of the breed. The dogs that are the closest to the Breed Standard will have a good show career, and their litters/stud services will be in demand as a result. This will lay down future foundation stock for the breed.

I have always claimed that, if the dog is good enough and campaigned enough, he will become a Champion, so stick with it if you do not have immediate success.

THE SHOW DOG
Throughout a show dog's career, he will encounter many situations: showing in rain, in marquees with sides flapping, in gales, in bitter cold, and in scorching sun. He will meet rough judges, nervous judges and, of course, gentle, kind judges. It follows that the show

The show Yorkie must be a typical specimen of the breed, with an outgoing personality so that it enjoys the rigours of the show ring.

dog must have the temperament of a saint and the stamina of an athlete to take all this.

Bathing and grooming for the show and the actual travelling can take several hours (see Chapter Six). There will be further grooming at the show, before entering the ring itself, where the dog must perform with aplomb and confidence. Finally, the tired show dog must be oiled and crackered before the tiring journey home. It always amazes me how show dogs adapt to all this; patience must be a trait bred into them.

COLOURING

The Yorkie's colouring is of the utmost importance if he is to become a Champion. At six months, the blue coat should still be quite dark, and the silken quality should be evident. The tan parts will still be quite pale, but with definite shadings. The colour of the hair on the ears often tells you how rich the tan will be at maturity:

- Pale golden ears   Tan but pale.
- Sooty ears   Solid heavy tan (and usually a woolly or 'cottony' coat).
- Rich tan ears   Eventual rich golden tan of the correct colour.

The quality of the silken coat varies, especially in different bloodlines. Some have the thick silk, others a thin sparse coat that does not thicken up until the dog is about two years old, and yet others have a wiry, hard coat that does eventually develop into a thick, silken, steel blue. All of this must be taken into consideration before you start the coat-growing process.

EARS

Some dogs' ears are slow to become erect; others have erect ears from birth. I have found this to be true if the ear is of the correct, small inverted 'V' shape. Large ears take time to become erect. To aid the process, remove the hair halfway down the ear on both sides so there is less weight on the ear. Massage can also help.

DAY OF THE SHOW

Your Yorkie should have been bathed the evening before the show. If he is a bad traveller, feed him as early as possible – he will travel better on an empty stomach.

Make sure you have with you:
- Your dog in his travel/show box, with bedding.
- Bedding for the bench.
- All grooming equipment.
- Food and water for your dog.

A grooming table is also very useful, and many types are on sale at shows. I recommend one with wheels, so you can load everything on it and pull the lot to your benching from the car park.

Arrive in plenty of time to settle your Yorkie and to exercise him. Groom your dog out in plenty of time for his class.

Hopefully, you have done all the ground-work. Do look at the other exhibitors with their dogs; you may think your dog is the best in the world but, up against competition, it can also be a 'pup'. Never be afraid to ask for help and advice from the most seasoned exhibitors; they are only too pleased to encourage new people in the breed.

As your class approaches, collect your box, brushes and, of course, your dog, and slowly make your way to the ring. If you are late and panicky, your Yorkie will become unsettled, and any nervous or agitated behaviour in the ring may result in losing an award.

Your exhibitor's number must be worn in a prominent position for the steward to mark you off in the catalogue and for the judge to see while judging. In AKC countries, exhibitors are usually given an armband bearing the number, which is worn on the left arm.

Line your box up in a straight line with the other boxes. Make sure you leave enough room between the boxes so as not to interfere with the exhibitors either side of you. AKC countries do not use boxes, stacking the dog on the ground instead. Most of the FCI countries exhibit on a box.

Stack your Yorkie in the correct position. He should stand four-square with his head looking at the judge. His topline should be level, and he should look alert, vivacious, well-groomed and have an air of importance about him. Brush him gently and reassure him in a soft voice (other exhibitors will not want their dogs put off by you).

The judge will walk down the line for an initial idea of the quality of the class – this first impression can often mean the difference between a high placing or nothing at all, so do make sure your Yorkie looks his best. Each dog in turn will be put on to the judge's table to be examined. His mouth, conformation, coat colour and breed characteristics will all be assessed. Never speak to the judge unless you are asked a question about your dog – such as his age.

When your dog has been examined, the judge will want to assess your Yorkie's movement, and will direct you to where you are to walk him (usually in a triangle and then up and down). To execute a good triangle, walk your dog away from the judge, with the dog on your left-hand side. The triangle is performed anti-clockwise. The judge will be able to assess the Yorkie's rear movement on the first part of the triangle; his outline and profile will be assessed on your turning left to complete the second part; and the front movement, head and expression can be seen on the second left turn as the dog walks towards the judge. The entire manoeuvre will also show off your dog's drive and personality.

When the judge has finished with you, return to your box ready for the judge's final decision.

PRIZES

If you are fortunate to have been awarded one of the five placings, the steward will guide you to the position wanted for the judge's line-up. In the UK, the judge will write a critique on

Practice makes perfect... a lot of hard work goes into training a show dog. This is Veronica Sameja-Hilliard with Ch. Verolian Out Of The Blue winning the Toy Group 3 at Crufts.
Photo: Carol Ann Johnson.

the first two placings, and this appears in the weekly dog papers. It is not obligatory for the judge to do this, but it is a matter of courtesy to the exhibitors.

In FCI countries, each exhibit is given a critique and grade. The grades range from 'Excellent' to 'Satisfactory':

Excellent	Awarded to dogs that fit the Breed Standard very closely.
Very good	Awarded to dogs of a similar quality, but who may have a few faults.
Good	Awarded to dogs who show the attributes of the breed, but who have breed faults.
Satisfactory/ Poor	Awarded to dogs who have physical faults, or whose appearance does not fit the Breed Standard.

In the AKC, the blue ribbon is given to a first place and a red ribbon for a second. The KC and FCI have red for first, and blue for second.

JUDGES

You will encounter many types of judges. As in every walk of life, some should certainly not be judging. If you arrive at the show and discover the judge is reputedly short-tempered, and if your dog is a little flighty, then avoid that judge at all costs, a lesson I have learned through bitter experience. As a judge myself, if I find a good dog upset, I will keep away and give it every opportunity. Handling your Yorkie with confidence will usually help him to overcome any nervousness.

Never try to hold a conversation with the judge, and remember his or her decision is final, even if you disagree.

REGULATIONS GOVERNING DOG SHOWS

THE KENNEL CLUB

The Kennel Club was founded in 1873, in effect as a 'gentlemen's club'. It is now the governing body of all 'dogdom' in the United Kingdom. The first Kennel Club show was held in June 1873. The KC took over the great Crufts Show in 1948.

It is with the KC that our Breed Standard is registered, as indeed are all the general canine societies and breed clubs. All the various types of shows have to be licensed by The Kennel Club, and The Kennel Club approves the judges who award Challenge Certificates (CCs) at Championship shows. These are the magical awards that allow a dog the title of Champion. To become a Champion, a dog must win three CCs under three different judges, one of which must be awarded when the dog is over a year old.

To exhibit at a show licensed by The Kennel Club your dog must be registered with the KC and you must abide by the rules laid down by the Club.

THE AKC

The American Kennel Club was formed in 1884, when it took over the records of an earlier organisation. Whereas the UK Kennel Club, as a governing body, is made up of individual people, the AKC is an organisation of member clubs. These clubs are elected to membership by existing members. Member clubs elect representatives to the parent club, which must approve them.

The AKC has elaborate and complex rules, which clubs must follow; failure to do so results in fines for the club. It also has field representatives to investigate reports of any fraudulent registrations, and may visit kennels to check that dogs are being adequately housed and cared for. They also attend shows to check that rules are being obeyed.

To show a dog (from six months), he must be registered with the AKC.

This organisation also licenses Championship judges, professional handlers, and dog shows, Obedience, Field Trials etc. The AKC maintains the Stud Books. The Breed Standard remains the responsibility of the breed club.

To become a Champion under AKC rules, a dog must achieve 15 points. How many points are awarded at each show is determined by the number of dogs competing, and the region in which the show is held. The maximum number of points a dog can win at a show is five points. Three, four and five points are classed as major wins. An AKC Champion must have two major wins under two different judges. One or two points are classed as 'minors'.

THE FCI

The Federation Cynologique Internationale was founded in 1911. The original alliance was between Germany, Austria, Belgium, France and Holland. It now includes most of Europe, plus Morocco, Mexico, Brazil and Argentina.

The FCI committee consists of a president, vice president, and sub-committees that are elected every year. Every three years, the general secretary, the treasurer and the three technical members are elected.

The FCI agrees the Breed Standard and Stud Books, controls shows, and deals with the recognition of international judges.

Am. Ch. Turyanne Rootin Tootin Tootin Jefre: Presentation and handling is of the highest standard in the American show ring.

For a dog to become a Champion in an FCI country, he must win three CACs (Certificat d'Aptitude au Championat). This will make him a Champion of the country in which he wins these three certificates. They must be won under three separate judges and there must be a 12-month gap between the first CAC and the third. CACs are only awarded at club shows.

CACIBs (Certificat d'Aptitude au Championnat International de Beaute are only awarded at all-breed Championship shows. To gain the title of International Champion, you must gain three CACIBs. There is no ruling about the time gap between awards.

Anglea Prophet with her extrovert showman Ch. Beezneez Tetley Bitter.

Kimevan Miss Monstruck – groomed to perfection.

JUDGING

Eventually, most exhibitors feel they have enough knowledge of the breed to want to start judging. You must have sufficient stamina to cope with what can be a demanding task, both physically and mentally. Once you are recognised as a breeder or exhibitor, you will probably be invited to a small show or match. If you would like to pursue a career in judging, contact your national Kennel Club for more information. Each canine governing body (e.g. the KC, the AKC, and the FCI) will have its own rules and regulations, and the method of qualifying is likely to change fairly regularly.

It is every judge's dream to gain Championship status eventually. This can be a long and demanding road, but, if you are knowledgeable and have a love for the breed, you will succeed.

When judging, you will be required to know the Standard and use it in evaluating the merits of each dog exhibited under you. Being a judge is a great responsibility, as judgements made will affect future bloodlines and so determine the quality and fate of the breed. You can withhold awards if you think the dogs lack merit. It is usually the first prize that is withheld, with second, third, fourth and fifth placings being awarded. If a judge fails to give a third prize, subsequent awards must be withheld.

When judging abroad, you must conform to the rules and conventions of the host country. You should be aware of any slight differences between the Standards, and judge to the one used.

10 BREEDING YORKSHIRE TERRIERS

To breed quality Yorkshire Terriers you will need to study the blueprint of the breed, the Breed Standard. You will also need a great deal of patience. Dog breeding is a blending of art and science, of your genius and a certain amount of good luck. It can also be expensive, time-consuming and heart-breaking; and, if you take it up seriously, it can be a lifelong commitment.

The successful breeder must judge the faults and strengths of his own stock, and eradicate any serious faults – through his breeding programme – to improve his own stock.

If you decide to breed, find out if there are any regulations you need to adhere to. In the UK, for example, you will need a licence from your local authority if you breed five or more litters during a period of 12 months.

THE BREEDER'S RESPONSIBILITY
All breeders want to establish their own line, i.e. a strain of related dogs who resemble each other closely. Never imagine you are going to make your fortune breeding Yorkshire Terriers. With the cost of stud fees, and of caring for the pregnant bitch (her whelping can result in an expensive Caesarean section), rearing her puppies, and advertising them, breeding can be an expensive hobby, with little – or no – profit.

Any breeder must be prepared to take back any pup or dog bred by them if an owner's circumstances change. It will be your responsibility either to keep the dog or to rehome him. Depending on the area where you live, it can be difficult to sell a Yorkie litter, resulting in you having to keep the puppies for some months. Luckily many people like an older puppy: he is past his baby days, is usually housetrained, and the potential owners can see more readily what size and temperament he has.

BREEDING PROGRAMMES

A basic knowledge of genetics can be of great use to the breeder. It is such a complicated science, that we will just concern ourselves with the very basics.

MENDEL'S THEORY

While growing peas, Augustinian monk Gregor Johann Mendel (1822-1884) discovered the laws of heredity and how characteristics pass down a generation. He discovered that inheritance depends on pairs of genes, which remain separate from each other and are passed unchanged from one generation to another.

By experimenting with his pea-growing, Mendel found that he could foretell the size of the pea plants, whether the peas would be wrinkled or smooth, and even the flower colour. He achieved this by crossing peas carrying certain features or traits. When two peas with different traits were crossed, one trait would appear in the offspring and the other would not. He called the trait that appeared 'dominant', and the trait that was hidden 'recessive'.

When the egg of a bitch is fertilised by the dog's sperm, this is initially one cell before multiplying. This cell

The rewards of breeding your own dynasty of Yorkshire Terriers. Pictured (left to right): Ch. Candytops Cassandra, Ch. Candytops Charmaine, Ch. Candytops Dream Lover and Ch. Candytops Amelia Fair.

contains 78 chromosomes, within which are carried the genes. The resulting pup will inherit 39 corresponding chromosomes from each parent. These 39 gene pairs and how they pair will be the deciding factor as to which traits the offspring inherits.

RECESSIVE GENES

Recessive genes need great consideration when breeding. They can remain hidden, and can be carried down the hereditary line, sometimes skipping many generations, until two dogs carrying the same recessive gene are matched. A subsequent mating will then bring this gene to light. The common characteristics caused by

recessive genes in Yorkies are: overshot and undershot jaws, lack of pigment on the nose, light eyes, small erect ears, long legs, and short heads. More often than not, it is the recessive genes which are responsible for the worst hereditary faults and abnormalities. In the Yorkie, these include: hare lip, cleft palate, congenital hernia, timidity, cataract, entropion, urinating when excited, and patella luxation.

If puppies in a litter show characteristics not visible in either parent – whether a defect or other characteristic – this will mean that both parents must have carried the recessive gene. If it is a defect, the parents should not be bred from again. It is also inadvisable to breed from any of the puppies.

DOMINANT GENES
Dominant gene characteristics are the traits we see: a dog will show the trait for a dominant gene, be a carrier of that gene, and be able to pass it on to his progeny. His progeny in turn will display the same trait and will be carriers. Dominant genes do not jump a generation. From observation, a good breeder will soon learn which genes are dominant and will be able to eliminate any dominant defects simply by knowing which dogs carry that gene.

No dog with health problems, and showing serious hereditary faults, must ever be included in any breeding programme. No successful kennel has

Ch. Clantalon Classified: The secret of a breeding programme is to build on your strengths.

ever been founded by breeding inferior stock. A golden rule for the beginner is never to mate two animals who appear to have the same fault, and it must be remembered that even the most outstanding stud dog will not be genetically suitable for all bitches.

IN-BREEDING
In-breeding involves the mating of two very closely-related dogs. It was used to produce the prototype Yorkie, but only the strongest and best stock were used. Unaware of the actual genetic make-up of their breeding stock, early breeders used dogs that displayed the traits required, which finally produced

Huddersfield Ben, the father of the breed.

It is essential to have a good knowledge of the dogs in the pedigrees and to be aware of their faults and virtues. An in-bred bitch is more likely to transmit her characteristics, be they good or bad, to her offspring, particularly if her mate is bred on similar lines. It is here that experienced breeders can be of great help to the beginner, as they will have in-depth knowledge of their own strains.

In-breeding increases the chance of the offspring inheriting the same genetic pattern from both parents: if both parents are outstanding with no serious faults, the offspring will be outstanding too; but hereditary faults can also be passed on, the results can be disastrous.

Father to daughter, mother to son, and brother to sister are examples of in-breeding. If this close in-breeding is continued for many generations, there is nearly always a size reduction, a loss of vigour, and a reduction in potency levels. A brother to sister mating can be successful – more so if one parent is outstanding – but it cannot add any new characteristics, and the resulting offspring will not be better genetically than either parent.

Any form of close in-breeding should only be done occasionally and for a special reason. The breeder who chooses to in-breed must be aware of any serious recessive faults in the strains and be prepared to keep or give away any inferior puppies, which should never be used for breeding.

In-breeding does not create bad genes, but it will make any hereditary defects very apparent, since closely-related dogs are more likely to have more common genes. If these genes are recessive (normally defective), it is not until two carriers are mated together that faults will become apparent. Hereditary defects are less likely to show when unrelated dogs are mated together.

LINE-BREEDING

This is the most common form of breeding. It involves the mating of related animals, but not those that are very closely related. This allows the owner to develop his own strain, with its own special characteristics.

As with in-breeding, the idea of line-breeding is to have a close common ancestor, or ancestors, of outstanding quality in the pedigree so that the line-bred dog is of exceptional quality. Line-breeding is similar to in-breeding but to a lesser degree. The same high standard in dogs used is required as in in-breeding. It can produce the same results as in-breeding, but not as quickly, and is far less dangerous. Line-breeding is the safest method of breeding for most, especially the novice and anyone with one or two bitches.

Any substandard dogs must not be used in any breeding programme.

OUT-CROSSING

This is the mating of unrelated dogs within a breed. It is usually done either to correct a fault, or to bring in new blood, or to introduce a particular trait from a different strain.

A single complete outcross on an in-bred bitch results in the progeny not being in-bred at all. The resulting puppies should be mated back to a dog of their own bloodlines, who shows the traits required. You cannot expect all the traits of the outcross sire to be in the resulting puppies. Some of his traits will be because of recessive genes, and, unless your bitch also carries the same genes, the puppies will not show these traits.

FOUNDATION STOCK

The most sensible way to begin your own strain is to buy a well-bred brood bitch and mate her back to her relations. Do not expect instant success from your pet bitch unless she happens to be reasonably bred. Founding a kennel this way can be a long process, fraught with disappointments. Select a mate of the finest quality, preferably a prepotent male (one who stamps his image on his progeny irrespective of the bitches to which he is mated). Not all his offspring will be his equal, but, by starting this way, you are on the right road. By line-breeding you can then establish your own strain.

BROOD BITCH

Your bitch should have certain qualities and be of a decent size, at least 4.5-6.5 lb (2–3 kg) in weight. Her breeding is all-important: not necessarily a show specimen, she should be free from any glaring faults in the breed. She should be as good as possible in her breeding and looks. Any bitch intended for motherhood should be kept in top-class condition.

The age at which a maiden bitch should be mated varies with her development. A brood bitch is generally at her best from 18 months to 6 years of age. In general, she should not be bred from more frequently than once a year. An overworked brood cannot be expected to produce top-class, healthy pups; she must be allowed sufficient time between litters to recover from the strain imposed upon her. A strong bitch, who has only reared one or two puppies and has lost no condition, may quite safely be bred from again at her next season.

A bitch comes into season for the first time at about six months, but it could be between eight and twelve months. Never mate a bitch on her first season.

As she starts her season, she will become restless, and will lick her vulva (which will redden, and become puffy and swollen). Over the next couple of days, blood will be discharged from her vulva. Usually blood-spotting on her bedding is evidence enough that she has started her season. This season will last

*Veronica Sameja-Hilliard with
the Verolian brood bitches.*

for 21 days. At about the tenth day, the discharge will change to a pink, watery discharge. She is now ovulating and, for the next few days, she will be receptive to any male dog in the vicinity, so will need to kept from any public places where other dogs may be present.

If you intend to mate her on the current season, contact the stud dog owner and book her in. Bitches vary as to when they need to be mated. The variation can be from 10–15 days; I usually mate them between the 12th and the 14th day.

STUD DOG

Anyone who owns a stud dog has a great responsibility to the breed. His qualities and faults will be passed on to future generations. Not only should he be dominant for breed type, but he should also be strong and virile, with an air of masculinity and a bold temperament.

It is a bad policy to allow the dog to be used frequently at public stud (that is, generally available to bitches of the right breeding) before he is fully mature. I usually use my boys at 10 months of age and then not again until 18 months. Using a youngster of 10 months gives him the confidence required to mate in the future. Always use an experienced bitch on a maiden stud, as she is the best teacher. The dog's character will dictate at what age you will allow him to be used at public stud. I do not generally put my show dogs to stud until their show careers are over. If used carefully, a stud dog should remain fertile well into old age and many Yorkie studs are quite capable of siring a litter at 14 years of age.

When deciding which dog to use at stud, you must consider not only the pedigree of the pair but also the traits you want to introduce from the dog. It is helpful if you can find out information regarding his background and hereditary traits, and he must certainly not show any of your bitch's faults. Many breeders can produce fine-quality Yorkies from just using their eye, assessing the virtues of the potential stud dog by what they see, and assessing the virtues of the bitch to be mated.

MATING

I always use a blanket on the floor for my Yorkies to mate on. All my boys, on seeing the blanket, immediately recognise it and become keen.

Let the potential stud out to relieve himself and to be ready for the bitch when he comes back in. He will want to play with her and will probably start leaping on her head, even trying to mate it! At this stage, try not to let him become too excited. Pick up the bitch if necessary and place her on the blanket, holding her gently at the head. Her tail will turn from side to side and she will position herself to receive the male.

As he enters the female, the dog's penis will enlarge considerably and the bitch will constricts her vaginal muscles to holds the penis in position. This is called the tie.

Ch. Ozmilion Dedication: Sire to Verolian Al Pacino and Ch. Verolian Out Of The Blue.

Once a mating is achieved, a maiden dog quite often panics at being tied to his mate. Reassure and praise him. After a few minutes, turn him so that they are back-to-back. You must now wait for his swollen penis to contract so that he can withdraw from the bitch. This tie can last from 5 to 45 minutes. Many successful matings have occurred without a tie, but most breeders prefer to have one.

When the pair separate, place the bitch in a towel to prevent excess sperm spilling everywhere and let her settle quietly somewhere. I do not like my Yorkie bitches to urinate for at least an hour after mating. Make much of the new stud dog, check to ensure his penis has retracted, put him back in his own quarters, give food and water, and allow him to rest.

A bitch always goes to the stud dog, as he will be more in command of the situation in his own familiar surroundings. If the dog does not perform, try him with a small feed first. I have one stud dog who will not mate a bitch successfully unless he has had a feed beforehand. If you are still having a problem, try lifting the bitch's front up a fraction off the floor. Make sure the stud is at the correct height for entering the bitch. This is where the blanket is so practical – you can fold it to adjust the height.

THE MOTHER-TO-BE

It will be 62–64 days before you see the results of the mating. Quite often, bitches whelp up to four days early and some (especially if the litter is small) one or two days late. This is normal.

For the next few weeks, the bitch can lead a normal life. As soon as you are aware of her being in whelp, increase her meals accordingly, and ensure she has a high-protein diet. At six weeks, it should be apparent that she is in whelp, depending on her size. Make sure she does not over-exert herself, and prevent her from jumping up and down on furniture.

Nowadays a bitch can be taken to a vet to be scanned. The vet should be able to tell you if the bitch is carrying puppies and may be able to give you an approximate idea of how many. This is not always a foolproof method, though: I know of many cases where people have paid large sums of money for a scan and have been told the bitch is not in whelp – and she then produces!

Personally, I find it much more exciting to let nature take its course. My own Ch. Verolian Wicked Lady, when mated to Ch. Ozmilion Dedication, showed no signs of pregnancy up to the final day. There was only a slight discharge from her vulva, which is usually a sign of a bitch in whelp, but, due to her normal size and antics, I was convinced she was not pregnant! She produced her singleton pup while I picked peas in the garden. The pup was

to be Ch. Verolian Out Of The Blue, top Yorkie for 1997 and 1998, Crufts BOB and Group Three 1998, winner of 23 CCs.

THE WHELPING QUARTERS

At seven and a half weeks, prepare your bitch's nest. This can be a purpose-built whelping box, a large cardboard box, a pen, or a large plastic bed. Whatever you choose, it must be large enough for her to be able to stretch out and accommodate her impending brood. Although it depends on the size of the bitch, a whelping box of approximately 2 ft 6 inches by 2 ft (79 cms by 61 cms) should be adequate. Situate it in an area of privacy, but near enough for you to keep a watch on her at regular intervals.

Warmth is a priority. I always have a lamp with a dull emitter at hand, which is ideal in the winter and on a chilly night during the summer. The new-born pups must be kept away from draughts and at a temperature of about 95 degrees F (35 degrees C), since tiny pups cannot control their own body temperature until they are two to three weeks of age. Do not overdo it, though while the mum and pups should be kept warm, they should not be cooked.

THE DELIVERY

Some bitches show nesting behaviour for up to two days prior to whelping but, as her time approaches, the mother-to-be will be restful and quiet. About 12 hours before, she may refuse all food. This is the best guide you can have. At this time, stay close by to be on hand. The bitch's bedding now consists of newspaper only, as this is absorbent and easily disposed of.

Signs of an imminent birth are:
- The renewed raking up of bedding (which can become quite frenzied)
- Panting
- Restlessness
- A general unsettled appearance.

The bitch will go quiet as her contractions begin; you will see her body ripple with the contractions, her tail raised as she strains and relaxes. Quite often, she will make low, yapping sounds or squeaks as her contractions move each pup down the birth channel into its new world.

This process can take a couple of hours. Be very watchful and keep nearby. The first sign that a pup is on its way is the arrival of the water bag, which looks like a small, dark, liquid-filled balloon. Quite often it recedes back inside the bitch as she pauses between contractions. This bag can appear up to two hours before the actual birth; any longer, and a veterinary surgeon should be summoned urgently. This also applies if the contractions weaken or cease completely.

As the first pup is expelled, the bag will break. It can break before the pup arrives, in which case I like the pup to follow pretty quickly. The pup arrives 'pre-packed', and the dam tears open the sac and severs the umbilical cord. Some do need assistance. The sac must be removed from the pup's face very quickly to enable it to take its first gasp of air.

If you need to sever the cord yourself, do it two to three centimetres (about an inch) from the pup, either by shredding it with your thumb-nail (taking care not to pull it away from the tummy and thus risk causing a hernia), or by tying the cord with cotton and then cutting it with scissors.

The new mother will clean the pup frantically, stimulating it to breathe and to seek out its first meal. During this frantic cleaning, the pup will also be stimulated to pass its first stool, the myocium. The placentas (afterbirths) will be eaten with great relish. I always let my girls eat them, and have found that, after three or four, if more pups are coming, they leave them. Do count the afterbirths – one for each pup. If they do not match the number of puppies, it means that one is retained in the womb, in which case your vet will need to administer an injection to get it expelled. Some placentas can take up to 15 minutes to be expelled naturally.

Each whelp should suckle as soon as possible since the dam's milk contains colostrum (milk that provides immunity against disease until they can build up their own resistance).

Await the next whelp. This can take two to three hours. As the next whelp is imminent, I always try to keep the

A completely unforeseen arrival: Ch. Verolian Wicked Lady with 10-day-old Ch. Verolian Out Of The Blue.

previous whelps away from mum's rear end, giving her space to manoeuvre and me space in case she needs help.

Some dams whelp quickly, some slowly; just be patient and vigilant. The last litter I whelped started at 4am and went on until 10pm. The process can take time and be nerve-racking for the breeder, but the dam takes it all in her stride. Be guided by your own instincts and your knowledge of your bitch. At this time, if the dam appears restful and calm as she prepares for her next whelp, you can offer a drink of warm milk. Don't worry if she refuses it – she's busy.

Finally, when the bitch has finished whelping, change the soiled bedding for clean. I let mum and new charges settle down for a couple of hours and check that all is well and that all the puppies are feeding. Some pups need to be put on a teat, but they should all be feeding well in a very short time.

After a couple of hours, put mum outside to empty herself; this is a very quick process, as her new family are very precious to her. Examine her very quickly, feeling her womb for a retained pup or afterbirth. Often, due to the process of whelping, a lump can be felt in her tummy; this is the contracted womb, not a pup. If the bitch is badly soiled, rinse her rear end, drying her quickly but thoroughly. Also check whether there is an afterbirth lying in the vulva. Quite often, in a large litter, afterbirths can get misplaced. If one is visible, gently pull it out. Put her back with her pups, with a welcome drink of warm milk. Depending on the time of year, you might want to turn on the heat-lamp.

FEEDING AFTER THE BIRTH

Solid food will be offered later. The dam probably has a full stomach of afterbirths at present, and, because of these, her next stool will be very dark and loose. For the first four days after whelping, her diet should be light and nourishing, so that her sore tum can recover. Offer chicken, fish and rabbit, with plenty of milk. When she has recovered from her ordeal, food should be on offer 24 hours a day. If she wants it, feed it. Water must be available at all times.

I give one calcium tablet daily, half in the morning and half at night. These are excellent and, since I have been using them, none of my bitches have had

Monitor your bitch's calcium intake while she is feeding her puppies. This litter is a week old. Photo: Steve Nash.

eclampsia. Some contain not only calcium but also vitamin D and phosphorus, to aid the absorption and utilisation of calcium.

POSSIBLE PROBLEMS

BREECH BIRTH

Many whelps are born bottom first. Act quickly if the bitch shows difficulty in pushing out the partly-born pup. Take a sheet or two of kitchen roll, grasp the pup firmly and, as the bitch has her next contraction, pull gently. The pup should slide out with ease. If it does not, the whelp must be removed very quickly if it is to survive. This sometimes involves a fair amount of force. As long as the pup is pulled in the correct direction, it should be fine. Some breech whelps need stimulating into life. Pat the pup dry and rub gently but firmly, holding the head downwards to clear any mucus and fluid in the lungs. A squeak will tell you when he is ready for mum, and she will do the rest.

CAESAREAN

With modern anaesthetics and all the latest veterinary equipment, this is a very quick and successful operation. Deciding to breed with the bitch again is a personal decision; if inertia was the cause, she will probably end up needing another Caesarean. If a puppy shooting up the opposite horn of the uterus was responsible, she should be able to give birth naturally. Discuss this with your vet.

The bitch will need great care and encouragement after her operation; she will go to sleep alone and wake up with a family of pups! Some bitches are horrified at the squirming pups, but they usually come round after a little encouragement.

If she is reluctant to take to her whelps, rubbing them with a placenta will induce her to lick them. Present her with the pups one at a time and encourage her to lick them, and, in no time at all, she will be settled with her new brood. I have never known a Yorkie to reject her pups.

The more the pups suck, the quicker the uterus contracts, which is very important to prevent infection or prolapse. The bitch will need care with her stitches; she has no idea her abdomen is stitched up. She must not jump or run back to her pups when put outside to relieve herself. With such precautions, her wound will heal very quickly, and stitches are usually removed after 10 days.

ECLAMPSIA

This is often called milk fever, and is usually caused by calcium deficiency. It affects the muscles, causing twitching and panting, which become progressively worse. Complete collapse can soon follow. This is a very dangerous situation, and a vet must be found immediately to administer a calcium injection. In the past, I have found that strangers visiting the house can induce an attack. I never breed from a bitch again if she has an attack, as I believe her daughters will also suffer from this scourge.

If eclampsia occurs, it is likely to develop either a couple of days or three weeks after the birth. This is when the hormone oestrogen is becoming active again, affecting her calcium levels. Increasing her calcium at this time can prevent it.

FADING PUPPIES

If your puppies start to cry incessantly and crawl around aimlessly, there is something wrong. Puppies do not cry unless they are in pain, or when they are hungry or too hot or too cold.

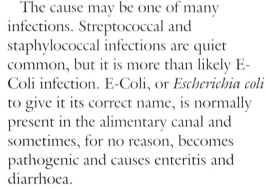

The cause may be one of many infections. Streptococcal and staphylococcal infections are quiet common, but it is more than likely E-Coli infection. E-Coli, or *Escherichia coli* to give it its correct name, is normally present in the alimentary canal and sometimes, for no reason, becomes pathogenic and causes enteritis and diarrhoea.

When picked up, the pup will feel cold and thin, and will appear 'pinched' and dehydrated. Strong puppies can build up a resistance, but smaller puppies invariably succumb and die after two or three days. Separating the sick pups and hand-rearing them may help, as may antibiotic injections. Any breeding stock must be of the highest calibre; any stock from sickly, poor breeding can never be regarded as a good prospect, no matter how well it may have been cared for throughout its life.

HAND-REARING

If, for some unfortunate reason, you have to hand-rear a litter, you will need stamina and patience. There are three possibilities: finding a foster mother, hand-rearing with a bottle, or feeding with a tube.

• **Foster mother**

Some bitches accept strange puppies very easily, especially if their maternal instincts are strong. Some will not be so easy, so the pups should be introduced

At two weeks old, these puppies now have their eyes open.

one at a time and rubbed with one of the foster mother's own pups. She will need to be closely monitored to make sure she has accepted them. If this still fails, remove the puppies and put them in a box with a couple of her own puppies – their crying should soon induce her to want them back, and, because the pups would have all rubbed together and mingled their scent, the foster mother should accept the entire brood.

• Immunity

Colostrum is the milk which the pup receives from its mother. It contains immunoglobulins, which protect the pup against all infectious diseases to which his dam herself is immune. Every pup should have colostrum within the first 24 hours of being born. I would suggest any puppies not receiving colostrum be vaccinated as early as possible to give them immunity against infectious diseases. All utensils used for

hand-rearing must be kept scrupulously clean.

• Feeding

Carefully read the instructions on the milk replacement tin and follow them The milk will need to be lukewarm. Do not add boiling water to it, as this will kill the vitamins. A new-born puppy is born with a strong instinct to survive, and will automatically suck, so the sooner you get him feeding, the better. Like babies, each puppy's intake of food will differ slightly. An average small pup will require a quarter of a pint (150 ml) a day, divided into several feeds.

You will need a foster feeder which can be bought from any good pet store. Small orphan puppies will need feeding little and often, about every two hours for at least a week. Some really small pups will need feeding for two weeks.

To feed the puppy with a feeder, gently squeeze the corners of the pup's mouth with your thumb and forefinger

A three weeks, growth rate is rapid, and the puppies need plenty of rest.

Photo: Carol Ann Johnson.

The first attempt at eating solid food.
Photo: Carol Ann Johnson.

to make his mouth open. Pop in the teat, making sure the tongue is under the teat and not in the roof of the mouth, where it would prevent him from sucking. To encourage him to suck, gently massage his throat or the sides of his muzzle. Be patient and do not feed him too fast, or milk could get into his lungs, which can be fatal. Satisfied puppies will look sleek and plump, their stools will be well formed and they will contentedly sleep between feeds.

• Tube feeding

If you need to tube-feed any runts, the vet will advise you on exactly how to do it. You will need a small syringe (10cc) and a tiny feeding tube. The tube will need to be marked to the length it needs to be passed. To do this, measure the length of the puppy from his mouth to

his stomach (three-quarters of the length to the last rib). With great care, pass the tube over the tongue and down the throat as far as your mark.

On no account must the tube be inserted into the puppy's lungs; this will be fatal if food is injected there. To test for this, put your ear to the end of the tube. If it is in the lungs, you will hear him breathing. If all is quiet, it is in his stomach. Once you are sure the tube is in the stomach, attach the syringe containing his warm food (to blood heat). Make sure there are no air pockets in the syringe, and slowly press the plunger and start to feed. Feed half the required feed, resting for a few seconds before finishing the feed. Withdraw the tube, wipe the puppy's mouth and finish off with the normal after-feed procedure (i.e. encouraging them to urinate and defecate).

Never overfeed. The pup's stomach should be extended but not tight. If it looks tight, he has had enough. Tube-fed puppies evidently do very well; not having to fight for their food saves energy, so their progress will be rapid.

It is a good idea to keep the hand-

The litter will feed from their mother until they are about six weeks old.

Photo: Carol Ann Johnson.

An evenly matched litter at five weeks of age. Photo: Steve Nash.

reared puppy wrapped in a warm towel when feeding. Not only does it preserve the pup's body temperature, it is also useful as a nappy and a bib!

If the puppies cry between feeds and their stools become yellow or green, dilute their next feed, or even give warm boiled water. It is very dangerous to let a pup become dehydrated. He will look thin and his skin will be wrinkled. A small puppy can quickly go downhill and it can be very difficult to revive him back to health.

After each feed encourage each pup to urinate and defecate. The dam would have licked these areas to stimulate the pup, but, by gently rubbing the areas with a moist piece of cotton wool (cotton), you will be able to encourage the pup to urinate. With a male Yorkie puppy, you will need to massage the cotton wool forward and along his penis; for a female, you will massage from the tummy along towards the tail. To encourage defecation, gently rub the tummy and anus.

Most hand-reared puppies become the most delightful Yorkies – being thoroughly spoilt and precious, a firm bond quickly forms between them and their new 'mother'.

INERTIA

This is when the bitch, after going through the preliminary stages of birth, actually settles down with no contractions and quite often appears very settled; or she may have been straining for a very long time, as a result of which the uterus has become exhausted. Veterinary help is needed immediately in either case. In the first case, the bitch will usually proceed with whelping after an injection by the vet; in the other case, a Caesarean is probably required.

MASTITIS

This is inflammation of a milk gland, occurring in bitches who have too much milk. Examine the bitch daily; any teat that looks congested should have a puppy placed on it to withdraw the milk. If the teats (it is normally the rear two) are red and feel hot and lumpy, literally milk the bitch. Get a

141

warm flannel, gently massage the teat, and then start to milk. Milk usually flows quite freely, and you may need to do this for a couple of days. If this does not work, she may have a bacterial infection, in which case she will require an antibiotic injection.

RETAINED AFTERBIRTH

If there is any doubt whether all the afterbirths have been expelled, a vet should examine the bitch and, if one is left, an injection of pituitary will probably be given to make the uterus contract and expel it. If the bitch starts panting heavily 12–14 hours after whelping, quite often she has a retained afterbirth.

DOCKING

Yorkies are customarily docked in the UK and the US. If no potential buyers have requested a pup with a tail, and you choose to have your puppies docked, this must be done by a vet four days after birth. At the same time the dewclaws should be removed.

PUPPY DEVELOPMENT

Your Yorkie puppies will develop very rapidly mentally and physically. In the first week, your pups will double their birth weight, be content and look fat and glossy. At about 14 days, their eyes and ears open and they react to noise and become aware of their siblings, dam and people as individuals. At three weeks, they start to walk, they can urinate and defecate on their own, and they start to play, growling, pawing and even wagging their tails. Their dam will leave them for longer periods and, with their new independence and so many things to do, they will not miss her.

Between four and five weeks, Yorkie puppies are becoming little individuals, playing games and busily sorting out the pecking order. A dominant pup will be quite apparent at this stage. They will come running to greet you and investigate any new situation. Toys and food are met with great enthusiasm. Their sense of smell develops after their eyes and ears are open. They will not intentionally soil their bedding and prefer to eat away from where they defecate; this can be of great assistance in house-training a young puppy.

By eight weeks, their teeth are through; they are now balls of black-and-tan fur, playing, fighting and eating. They are most amusing to watch. Often mum will still be checking them, disciplining them and keeping a watchful eye over them. Some bitches recognise their own offspring for many years and try to up-end them on meeting, even if their daughters are mothers in their own right. The delight of both in recognition is remarkable and a pleasure to watch.

The puppies will soon be ready to go to their new homes and bring years of happiness to their new owners.

WEANING

The puppies will gradually be taken off their mother's milk and new foods will be introduced until the pups no longer require food from their dam. They will normally feed from mum until they are six weeks old, while some dams feed their brood up to nine weeks, depending how strong the maternal instincts are.

We start to wean the litter at around three weeks of age. At this age the puppies can lap, and some may start to eat their mother's meal. This is a sure sign that they need extra food. Their dam is still sleeping with them at night, so trying to introduce a feed in the

morning is rather fruitless – mum's beaten you to it! I keep her away from them during the morning and, at about midday, give the litter a bowl of warm milk replacement. I place the pups round the bowl, and they soon show great interest and start their first laps. This can be a messy business. Often they will walk through it, stopping to lick their milk-covered legs. It is important to introduce one new type of food at a time to get the pups used to it and able to digest it.

The next step is to offer the extra food twice a day, increasing to three and then four times a day until, finally, they require no milk from the dam. After a

At eight weeks old, this puppy is ready to go to his new home.

143

week of being fed on their milk replacement for a couple of feeds, I introduce a feed of good-quality cooked minced (chopped) beef, which is always met with great relish. From then on, they will enjoy any meat feed offered.

Talk to your vet about when the litter should be treated for roundworm (it is usually at about five weeks). The dam should also be treated.

As soon as the puppies are put on food other than what the dam provides, she will become more disinclined to clean up after them and they will take less from her. She may regurgitate food for them at this stage – they will eat what they need and she will eat the rest. This is an instinct surviving from when their ancestors lived in the wild.

By the time the pups are seven weeks old they should be completely weaned. However, some dams are interested in their pups for many months to come, letting them have a quick feed (their sharp baby teeth being the only deterrent), playing and just enjoying their broods.

By the time the pups are eight weeks old, their diet should consist of four meals a day, and my own are fed as follows:

Breakfast: a complete puppy food soaked down.
Lunch (midday): repeat of breakfast.
Dinner (5pm): a meat meal of minced beef or finely minced tripe.
Bedtime: a drink of milk replacement.

If your litter was a singleton, weaning this only pup should not pose any problems. He probably won't move for six weeks, and will immediately take to his milk replacement and meat. Often, he will end up very spoilt!

11

BEST OF BRITISH

Mary Foster (also known as Mrs Jonas Foster) must be the greatest pioneer of our breed, bringing it to the public's notice and improving the quality.

Her Ch. Huddersfield Ben had produced many winning dogs for her, namely Little Kate, Bruce, Emperor, Sandy, Spring, and Tyler, and her Bradford prefix was known extensively.

From Ben's death in 1871, Mary Foster bred and showed many outstanding dogs, such as Toy Smart and Pride. As many new kennels were being formed, her stock was very influential in the development of the breed.

CH. TED

Sixteen years after Ben's death, Mary Foster purchased Ted, a four-year-old dog, at the Heckmondwike Show in West Yorkshire. Classed as one of the greatest little dogs of his time, and as a great influence in the breed's history,

Ted was born on July 20th 1883 by Young Royal ex Annie. Young Royal was by Old Royal, who himself was a son of Huddersfield Ben.

Ted had an excellent show career, winning 265 first prizes and specials. He was 17 inches (43 cms) from nose to tail, 9 inches (23 cms) in height at the shoulder, and weighed 5 lbs (2.27 kilos). He carried a wealth of coat, had an excellent head, and a dark blue colouring. Ted was quite short in the back by comparison to other Yorkies of the time.

Small dogs under 5 lbs (2.27 kilos) were desired by many breeders, and Ted was no exception. Dogs that were line-bred to him were small, and well-coated with good colouring. Obviously, like Huddersfield Ben, he also was prepotent.

Ch. Ted produced quality dogs. One in particular was Halifax Marvel (formally known as Aspinall's 'Teddy'). Halifax was the kennel name of Mr J.

Shufflebotham of Macclesfield. Marvel weighed 3³/4lbs (1.71 kilos), and had great coat and colour. He produced Halifax Ben (6.7.1897); Halifax Ben's brother Ch. Ashton Duke (5.6.1897); and Ch. Merry Mascot, (DOB unknown; became a Champion in 1898).

Halifax Ben weighed 3¹/2 lbs (1.70 kilos) and was rich in tan, with an excellent blue. He, in turn, produced Marvel Wonder (born 19.10.1901), who weighed 3³/4 lbs (1.71 kilos) and was also of excellent colour. The bitches that were producing these dogs were themselves bred on the lines of Ch. Ted.

EARLY 1900s

By the turn of the century, many breeders knew exactly the type desired, and realised that line-breeding was the only way of maintaining it. By using the dogs bred on Ted's lines, many excellent strains were forming: the Armley, Ardwick, Harpurhey, Sneinton and Pellon dogs are some of the best.

By the start of the First World War there were several important fanciers, but few people took a prefix and many show dogs came from unregistered parents, making it difficult to trace some pedigrees.

Sprig of Blossom, bred by Jack Wood (Armley kennels) and owned by Dick Marshall, is one such dog. From unregistered stock, her parents are reputedly King ex Minnie, born 3.6.1908. She gained her title in 1911, and was a big winner, reputedly having won 26 CCs, though records show only 21. A cup in her name is still on offer at the Yorkshire Terrier Club's annual Championship show.

Jack Wood's Armley dogs feature in many subsequent pedigrees and were very typical. Ch. Armley Little Fritz came from the Armley kennel and was owned by George Tomkins, who, with his daughter, Elsie, ran the Charleview kennel. This kennel was in existence up

PEDIGREE OF MARVEL WONDER.

Halifax Ben	Halifax Marvel	Ch. Ted
		Flemings Annie
	Crabtrees Lady	Halsteads Conqueror
		Robsons Bell
Marvel Queen	Halifax Marvel	Ch. Ted
		Flemings Annie
	Cannings Nell	Little Swell
		Ruby

146

A Yorkie of the 1900s.

until 1979, being first established in 1900!

1920 ONWARDS

The post-war years were far from being boom years for the Yorkshire Terrier, registrations only reaching between 150 and 200 per year. It was not until the early thirties that the Yorkie's popularity began to rise, and that registrations increased by about 50 per cent.

CH. LILYHILL SUPREME
Mary Lowrie (née Souter) took over the Lilyhill prefix from her aunt who died in 1921. Supreme was Mary's second Champion (1925), her first being Ch. Lilyhill Mademoiselle (1923). Her third Champion, Lilyhill Angelina, was the daughter of Supreme and Queen Mab.

CH. INVINCIBLE AND SPLENDOUR OF INVINCIA
Annie Swan's Invincia kennel produced dogs of excellent colour and soundness, and other breeders used her stud dogs and bitches to form their own lines.

Her first Champion was Ch. Invincible in 1927. His sire was Romily Jinks, (son of Conran Pride by Invincia Loopin, and both can be traced back to Halifax Ben) by Pillar of Invincia. In the stud book, his dam is entered as unregistered Peg. At this time, the Kennel Club allowed complete changes of name, so it is quite possible that there were two names for this bitch. Invincible won 14 Challenge Certificates and many Best in Shows. He weighed $3^3/_4$ lbs (1.71 kilos), had a good head, erect ears, with an excellent coat, a marvellous blue, and a rich golden tan.

Invincible produced five Champions: Ch. Gudasgold, Ch. Invincia Tini Blossom, Ch. Delite of Invincia, Ch. Eminent, and Queen of Perls (owned by Mrs Woodridge). From a repeat mating of Invincible came Ch. Mi Aroma in 1932. Ch. Delite of Invincia sired a great stud dog in Invincia Masher, but, due to the outbreak of war, he was never shown. In the post-war years – and just like his grandfather, Invincible – Masher produced five Champions: Ch. Splendour and Ch. Sunstar (both of Invincia), Ch. Adora and Ch. Hopwood Camelia (for Miss Martin), and Ch. Martinwyns Surprise

Ch. Splendour Of Invincia.

of Atherleigh (for Mr Coates).

The last Champion bred by Annie Swan was born in 1957 – Ch. Martini, by Ch. Splendour of Invincia ex Cherie of Invincia. She was the first Champion owned by Dorrie Beech (Deebees).

Annie Swan died at the age of 96 in 1975. She had a very long association with the Yorkshire Terrier to which present-day breeders are indebted.

1930 ONWARDS

CH. ROSE OF THE WORLD OF SOHAM

Lady Edith Windham (later to be known as Lady Edith Windham-Dawson following the death of her father), had her first Champion in 1929, Mendham Beauty (from the kennel of Mr W. Scolley). Soham kennels dominated the show ring through the thirties. From 1936 to 1938, of the 14 dogs which became Champions, 11 were owned by Lady Edith Windham.

Ch. Rose of the World of Soham (sired by Ch. Mendham Prince) took her title in 1932. She was a born show girl, with a wealth of colour and the correct coat texture. Champions Blue Bess of Soham and Thyra of Soham shared the same sire as Rose.

A bevy of Soham beauties.

CH. HARRINGAY REMARKABLE

This little son of Ch. Mendham Prince was considered to be one of the best of his time, with exceptional colouring. He took his title in 1933 and had a marvellous show career, winning 14 Best Toys in Show, 9 CCs and 200 prizes. At the Kennel Club show in 1932 he won the Kennel Club 'Send' gold vase for Best Toy and the Theo Marples challenge trophy for Best Non-Sporting in Show, the first Yorkie to achieve such great wins.

1940 ONWARDS

PARKVIEW PRINCE

William Bains of the Parkview Yorkies was an established breeder in Edinburgh whose dogs were true to type, with quality silken coats. He had the two brothers, Fairy Prince and Midges Pal, who were sons of Lilyhill Superb. Parkview Prince was a grandson of Fairy Prince on his dam's side.

William Bains' stud dogs, besides being of excellent quality, were to put their mark on the breed for ever by producing great Champions of their day. Prince produced Ch. Vemair Parkview Preview in 1949 and Vemair Principal Boy in 1951 (for Dr and Mrs Mair). Midges Pal sired Ch. Firhill Fairy, the Champions Tufty and Medium of Johnstounburn, and Vemair Spider (again for Dr and Mrs Mair).

Parkview Prince, when mated to Little Flea of Johnstounburn, produced the

Ch. Harringay Remarkable.

Ch. and Ir. Ch. Champion Mr Pimm of Johnstounburn.

IR. CH. AND CH. MR PIMM OF JOHNSTOUNBURN

Mrs Crookshank's famous kennel starts with Hazy, bought bedraggled off the street in Edinburgh for £5, and so began the little dog's long life in the luxury of the house and grounds of Johnstounburn, now a hotel south of Edinburgh. Hazy, who lived to be 17 years old, was brood size, with a very heavy coat. Her blue colouring was quite light, but she had an excellent clear golden tan. Her breeder was a Mr Notman, and her dam's side carried the blood of the Armley dogs.

Mrs Crookshank was persuaded to mate Hazy to Mr Bains' Fairy Prince. Hazy produced dams to Champions when mated to Fairy Prince or his brother Midges Pal. These matings produced: Misty, dam of Ch. Myrtle and Ch. Medium; Pixy, dam of Ch.

Ch. Mr Pimm Of Johnstounburn.
Photo: Thomas Fall.

Pipit; and Frosty, dam of Ch. Vemair Principal Boy. When mated to Midges Pal, Hazy produced Ch. Tufty (3.5.45), the first Ch. for Mrs Crookshank in 1949.

Meanwhile, a tiny dog (born 29.2.47) and his equally tiny mother had found their way to Johnstounburn, when their owner had died. This was 'Brownie' and his dam, Little Flea. With much care and love, Brownie was to become the immortal Ch. and Ir. Ch. Champion Mr Pimm of Johnstounburn. He was line-bred to Mr Bains' Fairy Prince and carried some excellent bloodlines.

Mr Pimm's lines can be traced back directly to Ch. Ted and then, of course, to Huddersfield Ben. He was a great influence on the breed and did much to popularise the Yorkshire Terrier, his photo appearing in many magazines.

As an adult, Mr Pimm weighed only 3lbs (1.4kg). He had a glorious steel-blue body coat, clear golden tan, and

was fine-boned. As his photograph shows, his topline was perfect, his head a dream, and he was all that the early pioneers of the breed had striven for. He won 5 CCs and 9 RCCs, as well as gaining his Irish title. He produced seven Champions: Myrtle, Pipit, Prim and Pimbron of Johnstounburn; Wee Eve of Yadnum; Buranthea's Angel Bright; and Buranthea's Doutelle.

The beautiful Ch. Pimbron of Johnstounburn was produced when a great-granddaughter of Fairy Prince and Hazy, Lady of the Lake, was mated to Mr Pimm. Pimbron was born 4.7.54 and was the last Champion Mrs Crookshank was to see; his title came in 1957, Mrs Crookshank died in July 1960.

Margaret Howes of the Seehow Yorkies, who was helping with Mrs Crookshank's dogs, had the unhappy task of putting to sleep all the 'oldies' including Ch. Mr Pimm, who was now 13, and his mother, Flea. This was at Mrs Crookshank's request.

Ch. Pimbron and his daughter, Minerva, were given to Mary Lowrie (Lilyhill), who took Minerva to her title in 1964. Pimbron produced two other Champions, a bitch for Mrs Wilson in Ch. Lillyhill Primbronette in 1966 and a son, My Precious Joss, for Mrs Christine Flockhart in 1965.

Some considered the Johnstounburn dogs a little too light in blue, but their quality and conformation far outweighed this, especially their ability

ABOVE: Margaret Howes, with four Johnstounburn Yorkies alongside a portrait of Mr Pimm.

RIGHT: Ch. Yorkfold Johnstonburn Gold Link.

to pass on their excellent traits to their progeny. They became the foundation for many future successful kennels, including Pagnell, Buranthea, Beechrise, Murose, Yorkfold, Whitecross, and, through the Ozmilion Champions, my own Verolians.

The Johnstounburn prefix is still in existence today, in the name of Daphne Hillman (formally Rossiter), who was granted it in 1982 from Margaret Howes (Seehow Yorkies), who had requested it from the Crookshank family on Mrs Crookshank's death. Minette, a daughter of Ch. Minerva of Johnstounburn was acquired from Mary Lowrie, and by line-breeding to Mr Pimm's progeny, Margaret still had the Johnstounburn strain to go with the prefix.

Since Minerva in 1964, there have been two Johnstounburn Champions:

Ch. Yorkfold Johnstounburn Gold Link in 1991, and Ch. Johnstounburn Gold Trim by Yadnum in 1997.

1950 ONWARDS

CH. YADNUM REGAL FARE

Ethel Munday started breeding during the late 1920s; it was not until the 1940s that the prefix was applied for and granted.

Ethel Munday made up seven Champions between 1952 to 1964. The first was Ch. Wee Eve of Yadnum, who was exported to America but was too small to be bred from. With her daughter, Vera Munday, at the reins from 1969, a further 11 were to take their titles.

Ch. Yadnum Regal Fare is one of the kennel's best. His sire is Ch. Candytops Cavalcadia ex Yadnum Lovejoy of

Ch. Yadnum Regal Fare.

Ch. Yadnum Certain Style.
Photo: Abbey.

Azurene. Regal Fare had a lovely personality, and was a fine example of the breed, his coat texture and colour being true to the Standard. He won 16 CCs, including Crufts in 1986, and was top-winning male in 1985.

CH. DEEBEES STIRKEANS FAUSTINA

This bitch, bred by Edith Stirk, carried the Invincia breeding. Her career was startling – gaining her title in 1958, she won 23 CCs in all. She was of outstanding colour and texture, had a pretty head and a super topline, and was a true showgirl.

Another outstanding girl was Ch. Deebees Beebee. A 1971 Champion, Crufts BOB and the Toy Group, she was exported to America to add American Ch. to her name.

Since the mid-1950s, 19 Champions have carried the Deebees prefix, the last

being in 1988. The kennel's foundation stock was Invincia.

1960 ONWARDS

CH. PAGNELL PETER PAN
Mr and Mrs V. Groom owned Prism of Johnstounburn, little sister to Ch. Prim of Johnstounburn. When Prism was due to be mated, she was taken to Ch. Burghwallis Little Nip, who was very much bred on the Invincia Lines (his father, Burghwallis Waggie, being a son of Ch. Splendour, and his mother being from the Lloyd-Worths' Rollerhome Yorkies). From the Prism-Little Nip union came two excellent Champions: a male called Burghwallis Vicki and a bitch called Pagnell Prima Dona of Wiske.

The next repeat mating resulted in Ch. Pagnell Peter Pan (17.10.1961), who was an outstanding dog, with beautiful coat colours and texture. Peter Pan was a BIS winner at an all breed Champion-ship show.

He was exported to Japan, and left three sons who all inherited his excellent traits: Ch. Pagnell Blue Peter, Ch. Heavenly Blue of Wiske, and the great Ch. Beechrise Superb.

CH. BEECHRISE SUPERB
Les and Hilda Griffiths bought Wee Taffy, their first Yorkie, in 1949. Mistress Anne, bred by Mrs Nunn from 'Of the Vale' Yorkies, was registered in 1951. When mated to Chants Bronte Janson, Mistress Anne produced the Griffiths' winner, Super Solitaire.

When a granddaughter of Ch. Splendour of Invincia, Amber of Beckanbee, was mated to Solitaire, they produced Beechrise Sensation. This dog, when mated to Beechrise Tina, produced Beechrise Pixie. Pixie was then line-bred to Super Solitaire, who appears as her grandfather, great-grandfather and great-great-grandfather. Pixie was also mated to Ch. Pagnell Peter Pan just prior to him being exported. This produced one of the breed's greats – 'Superb'.

Superb produced seven Champions from the 60s to the early 70s: Ch. Dandini Jim, Ch. Murose Storm, Ch. Gerjoy Royal Flea, Ch. Skyrona Blue Victoria, Ch. Toytop Tango, and Ch. Blairsville Aristocrat; and when Superb was mated to Jane Cutler (who carried Super Solitaire breeding too), his

Ch. Beechrise Superb.

seventh Champion was produced – the beautiful Ch. Beechrise Surprise, who went on to win 11 CCs.

Les and Hilda's kennel has always been known for producing dogs with excellent colour, conformation and beautiful heads. Les and Hilda were showing up to 1996 when Hilda died. Up until this time, they produced the following Champions: Swank, Shaun, Souvenir, Delstrom Music Maker and Status Quo. The only bitch to have the title is Ch. Beechrise Sweet Solitaire in the ownership of Margaret Sargison. Les is still very active in the breed.

MACSTROUDS WHITECROSS DANDINI
From the kennel of Jack Knight, and in the ownership of David Stroud, Dandini was to prove himself an influential stud. Bred on the Johnstounburn and Invincia lines, Dandini was to produce some great

Champions and bring instant success to the Chantmarles kennel of John and Mary Hayes by siring Ch. Chantmarles Mycariad Wilk Silk in 1968, Snuffbox in 1969 and Boniface in 1971.

By going back into the Whitecross lines through David Stroud's own Macstroud Champions, they produced the Champions Saucebox and Sashbox. By breeding their own dogs to each other and line-breeding them to Ozmilion Champions, further Champions were made up: Stowaway, Elegance, Dolly Dimple, Proper Madam, Celebrity, Best Intentions, Chivalry, Curiosity, and Gaiety. The Macstroud and Chantmarles dogs were responsible for providing the foundation stock for many new kennels, especially in Wales and the west of England.

Macstrouds Whitecross Dandini produced another Champion son, Ch. Dorrit's Macstrouds Hot Toddy for Dorris Baynes, who features in many pedigrees in London and the south-east of England.

1970 ONWARDS

CH. BLAIRSVILLE ROYAL SEAL
Brian and Rita Lister's foundation brood was Blairsville Lady. She was duly mated to a grandson of Ch. Burghwallis Vicki, Leodian Smart Boy (who had Invincia blood). From Lady's mating to Smart Boy came Ch. Blairsville Boy Wonder and Ch. Tinkerbelle.

Ch. Blairsville Royal Seal.

Tinkerbelle was mated to Ch. Superb to produce Ch. Blairsville Aristocrat, who was exported to Japan. One of his sons was to become the first Champion for the Ozmilion kennel, Ch. Ozmilion My Imagination.

Blairsville Belinda (out of Leodian Kandy Katy Verymuch Invincia, by Ch. Burghwallis Vicki), when mated to Ch. Boy Wonder, produced Ch. Blairsville Shirene in 1970. This bitch was mated to Richard Wardill's Ch. Whisperdales Temujin, to produce the dam of Royal Seal, Ch. Blairsville Most Royal. Most Royal herself won Crufts BOB, Toy Group and RBIS in 1974. She was a bitch of great quality and terrific texture, perhaps a little light for some, but sound and glamorous.

When the time came to mate Most Royal, she was taken to the Beechrise kennels to mate with the glorious coloured dog Ch. Beechrise Surprise. From this mating, she produced Blairsville Royal Seal, a dog of outstanding merit and a great showman.

Like his mother, Royal Seal won BOB, Toy Group and RBIS at Crufts, this time in 1978. It is he who claimed the breed record with 50 CCs, all under different judges. In his career, he won 12 BIS at All Breed Championship shows, 16 RBIS and 33 Toy Groups. He certainly was a legend in his own lifetime, excelling in conformation and coat texture. He had a beautiful head, was completely balanced and proved to be a great showman.

Royal Seal produced six Champions: Wykebank Startime and Wild Rose, Candytops Cavalcadia, Arlsestrey Regal Challenge, Jamessons Royal Stewart and Beebemi Blase.

Ch. Candytops Casper.
Photo: Abbey.

CH. CANDYTOPS CAVALCADIA

The Candytops kennel of Christine Crowther (formerly Oakley) has been very successful since the early 1970s. Her foundation stock was based on the Deebee's dog Candytops Deebees Peter Piper, who produced the first Champion in Ch. Candytops Blue Peter, in 1973. He, in turn, produced four Champions: Candytops Chantilly Lace, Strawberry Fare, Raffles and Candyman.

Ch. Blairsville Royal Seal was used in the breeding programme, and was mated to Ch. Chantilly Lace. This union produced Ch. Candytops Cavalcadia (15.9.1977), who was a very dominant sire, producing five Champions: Candytops Fare Delight and Royal Cascade; Wenwytes Whispers Boy (the first Champion for the Wenwytes kennel in 1982); Naylenor

Ch. Wenwytes Without Question: A grandson of Ch. Wenwytes Whisper Boy

Ch. Crosspins Brigadier.

Ch. Clantalon Classified:
Dog CC winner, Crufts 1996.

Crown Jewel (for Mr and Mrs Naylor); and Yadnum Regal Fare (for Vera Munday). From similar breeding came the Champions Candytops Royal Sovereign and Ch. Amelia Fare.

The introduction of Ch. Crosspins Royal Brigadier in 1993 produced the top bitch of 1996, Ch. Candytops Dream Lover. Four more Champions have been bred by the Candytops kennel: Ch. Katie Fare of Candytops in 1976, the sisters Ch. Cassandra in 1994 and Ch. Charmain in 1995, and Ch. Candytops Casper in 1998.

1980 ONWARDS

CH. CROSSPINS ROYAL BRIGADIER

Bred and owned by Jim and Pat Rigby in 1985, Brigadier was bred on the lines from their first dog, Bradstara Royalist, who was a son of of Blairsville Royal Monarch.

Brigadier was to sire five Champions: Ch. Crosspins Mory Kante, Ch. Royal Emblem, Ch. Candytops Dream Lover (for Christine Crowther), Ch. Beezneez Tetley Bitter (for Angela Prophet) and Ch. Patajohn Magic (for Pat Allington).

CH. CLANTALON CREDENTIALS

Douglas and Hannah McKay in Scotland founded their stock with Nelmila Berryfield Opal (of Ivy Millard), mating her to the Ozmilion Champions.

When Opal was mated to Roy Mulligan's Meadpark Personality Plus, she produced Credentials' father, Ch. Clantalon Contention. Their first winner features in Credentials' breeding too: Clantalon Notation (a son of Opal) was the first Yorkie to gain his Junior Warrant in Scotland.

Born in 1988, Credentials went on to

win 21 CCs and was top Toy in Scotland from 1990-1992. Another Champion male is Ch. Clantalon Classified, who, with Credentials and Contention, is a Crufts CC winner. Their current Champion is Connexion.

CH. AND IR. CH. OZMILION MODESTY

The famed kennel of Osman Sameja began in 1962 with two bitches, a daughter and granddaughter of Ch. Pimbron of Johnstounburn. In three generations of selective breeding to the Johnstounburn dogs, the first Champion was bred, Ch. Ozmilion My

Imagination, who was the start of the famed line of Champion males, all in direct descent: Jubilation, Distinction, Premonition, Tradition, Devotion, Ovation, Expectation, Invitation, Admiration, Dedication, Sensation, My Infatuation, Illumination, Mystification, and Sophistication.

The Champion bitches include the beautiful and extrovert Ch. and Ir. Ch. Ozmilion Modesty, who was a Jubilation daughter. Modesty's mother was a sister to Blairsville Aristocrat, Ozmilion Blairsville Bidene (Beechrise Superb x Ch. Blairsville Tinkerbell). Modesty won 19 CCs, Crufts BOB in

Ch. Ir. Ch. Ozmilion Modesty.

Ch. Ir. Ch. Ozmilion Jubilation.
Photo: Thomas Fall.

Ch. Ozmilion Distinction.

1975, and was the first big winner for the kennel by winning a Toy Group. She features in all the pedigrees of the later Ozmilion Champions.

Tragically, Modesty died at a very young age, and left a daughter by My Imagination. This daughter was to be Ch. Ozmilion Exaggeration, dam to four Champions: Tradition, Story of Romance, Flames of Desire and Invitation. Ch. Ozmilion Hearts Desire, a daughter of Premonition and Swedish, Finnish and Nordic Ch. Ozmilion Justaromance, was to produce five Champions: Ovation, Love Romance, Irresistible Love, Kisses of Fire and the great Ch. Ozmilion Dedication.

CH. IR. CH. OZMILION JUBILATION

The son of Ch. My Imagination and Ozmilion Justine, Jubilation was very typical. A tiny dog, weighing no more than 4 lbs, with a clear golden tan, his Johnstounburn blood was evident in his appearance. He would prove to be very prepotent as a sire by producing 14 Champions, including six Crufts CC winners, and becoming the top sire in the breed.

Jubilation produced the Champions Modesty, Distinction, Flames of Desire, Dance of Romance, my first Champion Ozmilion Dreammaker, and Ozmilion Destiny (for Mrs Montogomery), all bred by Osman.

His other Champion progeny are:

Kindonia Justine; Polliam Sweet Delight; Sladesmarks Sweet Allure; Chantmarles Celebrity and Best Intentions; Kerriwell Flirtation; my first bred Champion, Verolian Justajule with Ozmilion, and my bitch Ch. Verolian Temptress with Ozmilion, who was destined to become the record-holding bitch in the breed.

Distinction (Jubilation's son) was also bred on the Johnstounburn lines, his dam being a grandson of Ch. Heavenly Blue of Wiske. Distinction was an exquisite example of the breed – small (about 4 lbs), with great colours and a pretty head.

So began intensive breeding to the kennel's own stock to produce future famous kennels.

CH. OZMILION DEDICATION

Dedication, who gained his title in 1986, is the result of mating Ch. Hearts Desire (a granddaughter of Ch. My Precious Joss), to her grandson, Ch. Ozmilion Admiration. He became the breed record holder with 52 CCs, also winning 48 BOBs, 10 Toy Groups (including Crufts 1988, and two 2 BIS and 3 RBIS at all breed Championship Shows). He was also Top Dog All Breeds in 1987. He can only be described as an extrovert showman of great beauty with that true Yorkie character. His son, Ch. and Ir. Ch. Ozmilion Sensation, gained his own title in 1998.

In spite of never being at public stud,

of the few bitches he mated, he certainly made his mark on the progeny, and produced five more Champions: Ozmilion Elation and Signification; Ch. Rozamie Endless Love (for Brian Downey and Ralph Ensz), and Verolian Champions Al Pacino and Out Of The Blue.

Ch. Rozamie Endless Love, when mated to her half-brother, Ch. and Ir. Ch. Ozmilion Sensation, produced a big winner for them in Ch. and Ir. Ch. Phalbrienz Tamarix, winner of 22 CCs and14 BOBs, and Top Toy for 1991.

1990 ONWARDS

CH. OZMILION MYSTIFICATION
Born March 27th 1992, this boy was going to be a show-stopper: a fourteenth generation of home-bred male Champions in direct line, and his dam was a fifth generation of Champion bitches. He is 39 generations from Huddersfield Ben.

His sire, Ch. Ozmilion Illumination, had been mated to his aunt, Ch. Started With A Kiss. Mystification had two sisters in his litter: Ozmilion Love Forever was exported to Holland, where she gained her title; the other became Ch. Ozmilion Kisses For Ever.

Taking his first CC at 13 months in 1993, Mystification went on to dominate the show ring for the next three years. Along the way, he claimed 50 CCs (having failed to take the CC on just one occasion), 22 Toy groups, 3

Ch. Ozmilion Dedication.
Photo: Thomas Fall.

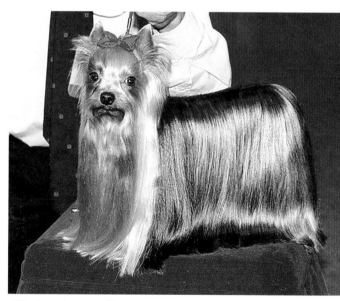

Ch. Ir. Ch. Ozmilion Sensation.

Ch. Ozmilion Mystification. Photo: Carol Ann Johnson.

BIS at all breed Championship shows, 7 RBIS at all breed Championship shows, Top Toy 1995, and Top Dog All Breeds 1996. In 1997, he took the title that had eluded the Blairsville Champions – the Supreme Champion at Crufts. The same day, he was retired from the show ring. Still in his prime, with a wealth of coat of glorious rich colour, and showing magnificently, it was decided that Mystification could achieve no higher accolade. For the rest of the year, Osman took Mystification out to public events, so that those who had not yet seen him could do so and appreciate his many qualities.

With nearly 40 Ozmilion Champions and further breeding, we can expect more to come. This is the only kennel to have bred five Champions who have won Best in Show at all breed Championship Shows. Many breeders use the Ozmilion dogs to produce their own Champions and to improve their stock.

Ch. Verolian Temptress With Ozmilion.

Ch. Verolian Justajule.

CH. VEROLIAN TEMPTRESS WITH OZMILION

My first Champion was Ch. Ozmilion Dreammaker in 1976. Dreammaker and my Ozmilion Wild Temptress (Ch. Imagination and granddaughter of Ch. My Precious Joss) are the foundation girls for my kennel. Wild Temptress produced my first male Champion (when mated to Jubilation), Justajule With Ozmilion. Justajule was not a tiny dog, but was so very sound. He carried a wealth of coat and, like his ancestors, the golden clear tan.

A true gentleman, he was a great influence on my breeding stock and produced my Ch. Verolian the Adventuress at Ozmilion. She was to produce two Champions for my kennel: Al Pacino and Wicked Lady. My Dreammaker had produced a daughter by Ch. Ozmilion Premonition whom I had given to Osman; she was Ozmilion Love Story.

Ch. Verolian Kitten On The Quays.

She returned to me in 1980, mated to Ch. Jubilation and produced 'Sarah', who was registered Verolian Temptress. Because of my close association with Osman, 'With Ozmilion' was added to her name. With her qualities, Sarah was to tempt many.

After a slow start, Temptress blossomed. She took her first CC in October 1982, and won every CC and BOB for the rest of that year. She won the Crufts CC and BOB in 1983, and, by the end of the year, she had accumulated 23 CCs and the Top Yorkie title. We didn't attend Crufts in 1984, as Osman was judging, but that year she won more CCs and BOBs, to finish the year with a total of 39 CCs, taking the Top Yorkie title again and also that of Top CC Winning Bitch in the breed.

A Temptress daughter, Verolian Huntress, by Ch. Ozmilion Admiration, when mated to my Ch. Al Pacino, produced my top bitch of 1994 and Crufts CC winner – Ch. Verolian Kitten On The Quays.

CH. VEROLIAN OUT OF THE BLUE

This young lady, from my Ch. Verolian Wicked Lady out of Ch. Ozmilion Dedication, was an extrovert with a glorious colour. Born July 3rd 1994, she won 23 CCs, Crufts BOB in 1998 and Group 3, and Top Yorkie in 1997 and 1998.

Thanks to the Ozmilion dogs providing me with an excellent gene pool, I have been fortunate enough to produce my lovely Champions.

CH. PHALBRIENZ FLORIBUNDA

Messrs Brian Downey and Ralph Ensz, took on the challenge to show Flori (7.8.91) undocked. It was not done as a protest against docking – it just happened that their vet was on holiday when she was born. She was kept with the intention of being a brood bitch, but, as she grew, she exhibited great potential as a show girl, and rewarded them in 1993 by gaining her title.

Sired by Swedish Ch. Ozmilion Revelation (out of Phalbrienz Blue Veil) she became the first, and, to date, the only undocked Yorkie Champion in the UK.

12 THE AMERICAN YORKIE

By Betty Dullinger

Although the breed began in the Yorkshire district of England, its fame very quickly spread to other parts of the world, and some were exported to the US in the latter part of the 19th century. Most of the breeders of that early time resided on either the East or West Coast, with only a few in the mid section of the country, which is mostly farm and grazing land, and thus more suited to the larger working breeds of dogs. The little Yorkshire Terrier became popular in the larger cities, particularly among the fashionable ladies of the era.

Yorkshire Terriers were being exhibited at dog shows in the late 19th century and their stylish good looks, cocky attitude and long, shimmering coats of blue and gold brought them immediate praise and popularity. Figures indicate that 48 Yorkshire Terriers were registered in 1890; 80 in 1913; 40 in 1924; 78 in 1934; and 49 in 1944. Following the war, the

From its early beginnings, the Yorkshire Terrier was quickly adopted as a popular show dog and companion in America.

registration figures took a meteoric rise: to 173 in 1949; 1,181 in 1960; 13,484 in 1970; 24,665 in 1980; and 42,900 in 1998.

Some early breeders of note included:

Goldie Stone, whose Petit Kennels in Ohio produced many winners in the 30s, 40s and 50s and, in fact produced the first American bred Yorkie to win a Best In Show, Ch. Petit Magnificent Prince.

Mr and Mrs Arthur Mills (Millbarry) were active in the 40s and 50s. They imported three very important dogs from England: Ch. Fritty, Ch. Miss Wynsum and Ch. Suprema. Ch. Miss Wynsum was the first Yorkie to win the Toy Group at Westminster. Ch. Suprema won two Groups in her show career and sired seven Champions, one of which was Ch. Milbarry's Sho Sho, which was the second Yorkie to win the Toy Group at Westminster. Ch. Fritty became the mascot of the Yorkshire Terrier Club of America (YTCA) and was the model used for the club pin which is worn by many of the YTCA members today.

Mrs Paul Durgin of Minnesota was also influential in the 40s and 50s. She owned the imported Pretoria Action (English and Irish Ch. Twinkle Star of Clu-Mor x Connie of Lauderdale). Action's daughter, Caroline of Clonmel was the dam of Clarkwyn Miss Debutante, Wildweir Butterscotch and Wildweir Lollipop.

Kathleen Kolbert of Turyanne Kennels, Connecticut, began breeding Yorkies in 1965 and showed her first Yorkie in 1968 at the First Company Governors Foot Guard show in Hartford, Connecticut, under judge William Kendrick, who awarded Lord Pickwick of Oxford Winners Dog and Best of Winners. Pickwick went on to finish his Championship in 1968 with three major wins. He produced five Champion offspring and each of these has gone on to produce Champions.

The kennel gets its name from the family homestead which was known as Tury's Tavern, a well-known stage stop for the weary traveller. The house was part of the underground railway and had a secret place in the chimney for hiding slaves. The kennel name has been registered with the American Kennel Club for the past 25 years. Kathleen has bred several dogs that have made great contributions to her lines. One of these was Ch. Always Love De Penghibur ROM, also known as Louie.

Louie, Ch. Easy James De Penghibur and Ch. Huddersfield Ben De Pengibur were all brothers that Turyanne has used at stud over and over again and are now producing children, grandchildren and great-grandchildren who are all finishing their Championships and making their mark with group placements.

Am. Ch. Lord Pickwick Of Oxford.

Am. Ch. Always Love Damion.
Photo: The Standard Image.

Turyanne Always Love Jason.
Photo: The Standard Image.

Ch. Always Love De Penghibur ROM sired a litter of three Champions: Ch. Turyanne Always Love Hobie, Ch. Turyanne Always Love Hunter and Ch. Turyanne Always Love Harley. Hobie was the sire of World Champion and American Champion Hooligan De Penghibur, who was a Specialty winner in the US and a Best in Show winner several times.

Barbara and Ron Scott established Stratford Yorkshire Terriers in 1983. The name 'Stratford' was chosen because the area they lived in at the time was Stratford Manor, a suburb of Pittsburgh, Pennsylvania.

The Scotts have bred and exhibited Yorkies for 16 years with their foundation based on their first bitch, Ch. Denaire Royal Lace ROM, daughter of an English import, Ch. Royal Icing (who produced 36 Champions) and Ch. Denaire Fame (who produced 11 Champions). Ch. Denaire Royal Lace ROM produced seven Champions and her son, BIS/BISS Ch. Stratford's Magic ROM, and grandson Ch. Stratford's Blue Max, were to become Stratford's top-winning dogs, both multiple Best in Show and Best in Specialty Show winners.

Over the years, the Scotts have achieved 60 American Champion titles, (48 bred by the Scotts). They were the recipients of the following awards from the Yorkshire Terrier Club of America:
• 1991 and 1992 Top Winning

Am. Ch. Denaire Royal Lace ROM.

BIS/BISS Am. Ch. Stratford's Magic ROM.

Yorkshire Terrier – BIS/BISS Ch. Stratford's Magic ROM.
• 1994 and 1995 Top Winning Yorkshire terrier – BIS/BISS Ch. Stratford's Blue Max.
• 1995 Top Breeder: Stratford – Barbara and Ron Scott.
• 1997 Top Producing Dam – Ch. Stratford's Heaven Sent ROM.
• 1997 Top Producing Sire – BIS/BISS Ch. Stratford's Magic ROM.
The Scotts have also had seven bitches and two dogs who have earned their YTCA Register of Merit award for being top producers.

Three of Stratford's most recognised Yorkshire Terriers were: BISS Ch. Mistangay Boom Boom Mancini ROM, BIS/BISS Ch. Stratford's Magic ROM, and BIS/BISS Ch. Stratford's Blue Max.
• BISS Ch. Mistangay Boom Boom

Mancini ROM (16.3.85 - 21.7.99): Bred by Renee Emmons, Boom Boom got two Best in Specialty Shows, five Group firsts, 24 Group placements, and 54 Best of Breeds (specialed eight months). He sired six Champions.

• BIS/BISS Ch. Stratford's Magic ROM (22.4.86 –)
Bred by Barbara and Ron Scott, Magic's achievements include: No.1 Yorkshire Terrier 1988 (Routledge and Chronicle), No.1 Yorkshire Terrier 1991 and 1992 (Yorkshire Terrier Club of America), 1992 Best of Breed (Westminster Kennel Club), in Top Ten Rankings five years in a row, three Best in Shows (All Breed), six Best in Specialty Show (Yorkshire Terrier Club of America National 1994), 61 Group firsts, 178 Group placements, and 266 Best of Breeds.

BISS Am. Ch. Mistangay Boom Boom Mancini ROM.

• BIS/BISS Ch. Stratford's Blue Max. Max's achievements include: 1994 Pedigree Award Winner, No.1 Yorkshire Terrier 1994 and 1995 (Yorkshire Terrier Club of America), five Best in Shows (All Breed), five Best in Specialty Shows (Yorkshire Terrier Club of America National 1994), 61 Group firsts, 178 Group placements, and 266 Best of Breeds. He sired four Champions.

FIRST AMERICAN YORKIE CLUB
In 1951, with registration figures steadily rising, some of the important breeders of the era decided that a club should be formed to protect the breed. The Yorkshire Terrier Club of America was the result of those efforts and thus the club was chartered in California. A Code of Ethics to guide breeders, as well as by-laws, were drawn up by the founding members; some years later, the YTCA applied for and was granted membership status in the AKC (American Kennel Club). There are at present only two Charter members of the YTCA who still remain members today: Joan B. Gordon (Illinois) and Bill Wynne (Ohio).

At present the club boasts a membership of 500, holds at least one annual Specialty show, has a stringent Code of Ethics and a recently added Code of Conduct to which all members are expected to adhere. To gain membership into the YTCA an applicant must be sponsored by two members who have known the applicant for at least two years, and at least one of the sponsors must have visited the applicant's home/kennel in the past year. Dues and an initiation fee are collected, the application is reviewed by the club's membership committee, the applicant's name is published in the *Yorkie Express* (the quarterly club magazine) and, following publication, is voted on by the board of directors.

The Club also gives a title – a Register of Merit (ROM) – to dogs who have sired six or more Champions, and bitches who are the dams of three or more Champions.

SOME YORKSHIRE TERRIER GREATS

All of the dogs and breeders I have chosen to cite are not only examples of excellent Yorkshire Terriers, but have all made significant contributions to the breed in the United States. Their owner-breeders are all dedicated to improving the breed by breeding only sound, healthy dogs which epitomize the very essence of the breed and its character.

CH. LITTLE SIR MODEL (1949-1962)

An import from England, owned by Wildweir Kennels of Joan B. Gordon and Janet Bennett, Ch. Little Sir Model was the first Yorkie in the US to win an all-breed Best In Show. Ch. Little Sir Model was based on Pellon and Armley lines, which trace back to Huddersfield Ben through his grandson Ch. Ted. Little Sir Model, when bred to a bitch of Clu-Mor breeding, produced Ch. Proud Girl of Clu-Mor, who was the first bitch to win an all breed BIS. Wildweir has had many more BIS winners since their beginning in 1949.

CH. STAR TWILIGHT OF CLU-MOR ROM (1950-1962)

Another early winner for Wildweir, 'Tuffy' boasted 103 Best of Breeds; 26 BIS; 86 Group Firsts; and 22 Group placings. Every time Tuffy won the Breed, he either also won or was placed in the Toy Group – quite a remarkable feat. He was the BIS record holder in the breed until Ch. CeDe Higgins, his great-great-grandson took over the record.

Am. Ch. Star Twilight Of Clu-Mor ROM.

Tuffy was also the Best of Breed winner at the first five YTCA Specialties. He won two consecutive Group Firsts at Westminster Kennel Club and was placed second in the Group the third year he was shown there, being defeated in the Toy Group by the Toy Poodle which susequently was placed BIS!

Tuffy was the sire of 15 Champions and holds an ROM title. In the early 1980s a ceramic likeness of Tuffy was created by Anne Seranne which was used for trophies in all the classes at the YTCA Specialty.

Ch. Star Twilight of Clu-Mor set the

stage for the style of our modern-day Yorkies. He was of correct size and proportions, with the correct colour and texture of coat. His beautiful head and outline made him an outstanding specimen of the breed, and, were he alive today, he could still be competitive in today's show ring.

CH. WILDWEIR POMP N' CIRCUMSTANCE ROM (1959-1972)
Pompey was a double grandson of Ch. Star Twilight of Clu-Mor, being the result of a half-brother half-sister mating. He is the top sire in the breed, having sired a total of 95 Champions. This is truly a remarkable number of Champions when one considers that shipping by air was not as prevalent as it is today and Wildweir insisted that the owner bring the bitch to them for breeding.

Pompey figured prominently in the bloodlines of most of the major kennels of the 60s and 70s, among them Northshire (Dorothy and Walter Naegele), Kajimanor (Kay and Nelson Radcliffe), Clarkwyn (Ila Clark), and Bridlebar (Barbara West Clark).

The kennel name Wildweir is taken from the children's book *The Wind in the Willows*. Joan Gordon is the only living prominent breeder with 50 years of experience in Yorkies. The Wildweir kennels bred or finished 245 Champions, and there are five more with points waiting to be finished. Wildweir is now owned by Joan B.

Am. Ch. Wildweir Pomp N' Circumstance ROM.

Gordon and Nancy C. Donovan. All Wildweir dogs were owner-handled to their Championships.

AM., CAN., BDA., MEX. CH. NORTHSHIRE MAZEL TOV ROM (1967-1980)
'Ollie' was bred by Dorothy and Walter Naegele (Illinois), and was an important stud dog of the 70s, appearing in many pedigrees of that era. He sired 35 Champions. In the ring he was always shown by his breeder/owner Dorothy, and was the winner of 10 Groups and 27 Group placings in the US; two Groups in Canada and two Groups in Bermuda. He was Best in Specialty Show at the Yorkshire Terrier Club of St Louis in 1974, achieving this honour from the Veteran Class (for dogs and bitches seven years and older).

At the same show he was also named Best Stud Dog, being shown in that class with six of his Champion offspring.

Dottie Naegele started showing in 1962 when she had Toy Poodles. She got her first Yorkie the same year and shortly thereafter started showing and breeding Yorkies. She has bred 50 Yorkshire Terrier Champions (and five Shih Tzu Champions).

In 1972, Dottie applied for and received her licence to judge Yorkies. She is currently licensed to judge all breeds in the Toy Group (Group V), all varieties of Poodle, and BIS. Dottie continues to judge, and, as of late 1998, started out a new puppy in the show ring, which is now pointed.

CH. CEDE HIGGINS ROM (1973-1983)

Higgins is the only Yorkie to win the coveted title of BIS at the prestigious Westminster Kennel Club show in New York. This feat was accomplished in 1978, and the judge was Anne Rogers Clark.

Higgins was bred by C.D. Lawrence, owned by Bill and Barbara Switzer and shown by their daughter, Marlene Lutovsky. Higgins was a very stylish little dog of correct size with a beautiful, silky coat and an incomparable personality that won friends for both him and the breed wherever he went.

No one will ever forget Higgins and Marlene, and the way she would play ball with him in the ring while they were awaiting their turn to be judged. Higgins was the winner of several Yorkshire Terrier Specialties, innumerable Groups and BIS at all breed shows.

Higgins was used very sparingly at stud, so many breeders bred to his sire instead, Ch. Clarkwyn Jubilee Eagle ROM, who became a top producer.

Marlene always used red polka dot bows on Higgins; this became a trademark of sorts and thereafter many other exhibitors started using polka dot bows on their Yorkies' topknots.

CH. CLARKWYN JUBILEE EAGLE, ROM (1970-1983)

Bred by Mrs Ila Clark from Seattle, Washington, and owned by Ruth Jenkins from Issaquah, Washington. In the late 70s and early 80s 'Jubie' exerted a major influence in the breed. Not only did he sire the famous Ch. CeDe Higgins ROM, but he also sired Ch. Fardust Fury, owned by the late Dustine Bitterlin who was another Specialty winner. Ch. Jentre's Charger of Mistangay ROM was another Jubie offspring that excelled as a stud dog.

After Higgins' BIS at Westminster (commonly referred to as The Garden), his stud fee became prohibitive for most breeders; so instead breeders took bitches to Jubie, his sire, or to Charger, his half-brother.

CH. JENTRE'S CHARGER OF
MISTANGAY ROM (1977-1990)
Bred by Ruth Jenkins, and owned by
the late Renee Emmons, from Atlantic
City, New Jersey. Renee purchased
Charger in the late 70s from Ruth
Jenkins. He was successfully shown to
his Championship by his owner. He
excelled as a stud dog and sired 35
Champions, two of which became top
winners and producers: Ch. Rothby's
Reneegade ROM and Ch. Caraneal's
Charged and Ready ROM. Charger
figures prominently in the bloodlines of
many Yorkshire kennels and it is not
unusual to see Charger in the pedigree
more than once of many of today's top-
winning dogs from coast to coast.
Bobbi Rothenbach named her Rothby's
Reneegade (Gator, see below) as a
tribute to Renee who was suffering
from the cancer which later took her life
at a young age.

*Am. Ch. Jentre's
Charger Of
Mistangay ROM.*

CH. ROTHBY'S RENEEGADE ROM
(1984-1998)
A very recent top producer, 'Gator' was

bred, owned, and handled to his
Championship by Bobbi Rothenbach,
from Rothby's kennels. Bobbi has been
breeding Yorkies for 30 years, and
bought her first Yorkie back in 1965.
Her kennel name, Rothby, is a
combination of her married name
(Rothenbach) and her maiden name
(Ashby).

In his show career Gator won three
consecutive National Specialties, a total
of five Yorkie Specialties and three all-
breed BIS. Gator is best known for the
style that he stamped on all of his
puppies; that style is still evident in his
grandchildren and great-grandchildren.
He has produced a total of 83
Champions to date, of which 13 are
ROM recipients. His top-winning son,
Ch. Rothby's Reputation ROM, is the
sire of 10 Champions to date and was
recently retired with four all-breed BIS
and 24 Yorkshire Terrier Specialties,
under 23 judges.

Rep is the youngest Yorkie to win an
all-breed BIS (at just 22 months of age)
and was the Pedigree Award winner in
1997 and 1998. Rep was also always
breeder-owner handled.

Gator contributed to many of the top
bloodlines of the day, most notable are:
Durrers (Betty Anne and Richard
Durrer) breeders/owners of Am., Can.
Ch. Durrer's Ace High ROM, Canada's
top-producing Yorkie.

Majestic (Carole Klein) Ch. Rothby's
Majestic Pride N Joy ROM, a Gator

*BIS/BISS Am. Can. Ch.
Rothby's Reneegade ROM.*

granddaughter who has produced a
Specialty winner and the top winner in
France when she was bred back to
Gator.

Parkside (Dr Ivan and Marie Kaufman-
Cardona) Ch. Parkside Safari ROM.
Safari, a Gator grandson is Parkside's
top producer and consequently is
represented in most of the top winners
of Puerto Rico, Central America,
Mexico and South America.

Du Gene De L'Adour (Yvonne Jan
and Catherine Consten) Int. Ch. BIS
Puerto Rico, Am. and French Ch.
Majestic Monarch, top Yorkie in France,
1998, co-owned by Marie Kaufman-
Cardona, bred by Carole Klein. A Gator
son, Danny is being used at stud
extensively in Europe.

Pennylane (Barbara Irwin) has two
Specialty winning brothers sired by
Gator: Ch. Pennylanes On The Target
and Ch. Pennylanes Blu Chip Nugget.

Exmoor (Jim Hupp and Brett Walker)
BIS, BISS Ch. Exmoors' One Better
ROM, was the top-winning bitch four
consecutive years 1991-1994, as well as
a top producer. 'Monie' is Gator's top-
winning daughter.

Diamond T (Lezle Treadwell), BISS
Ch. Rothby's Diamond T Darci ROM,
a Gator daughter.

Stratford kennels (Barbara and Ron
Scott) Ch. Rothby Stratford Showgirl
ROM and Ch. Stratford the Magician
ROM are top producers and are Gator
grandchildren.

Jo-Nel kennels (Julie Howard) has
several Champions who are either Gator
children or grandchildren. Julie's top-
winning bitch, Ch. Jo-Nel's Pen-EZ
from Heaven is a Gator granddaughter.

Mary Nehf owns the current top-winning Yorkie, Ch. Sterling's Wild Card O'Marne. Oliver is a Gator grandson and is shown by his breeder Kay Joiner.

Lazron (Sharon Horzsa), **Traces** (Cheryl Rangel), and **Willobar** (Sue Barbour) all got their foundation stock from Rothby and now co-own several dogs with Bobbi. **TeaTime** (Linda Velasquez) has at least three generations of Rothby-based Champions.

CH. YORKBORO CRIMSON AND CLOVER ROM (1979-1995)

Clover (bred and owned by Doreen Hubbard) was never bred to the same male twice, but was always line-bred within Clarkwyn and Mayfair bloodlines. She was a daughter of Ch. Mayfair Barban Jamoca ROM and Oaksaber Gold Confetti. Her last two litters resulted from breeding to her grandsons and it was this linebreeding which served to establish the type for which Yorkboro is known.

Clover's dam was a daughter from the breeding of Ch. Clarkwyn Double Eagle, 1974 National Specialty winner and an English import of the Fayre and Capella lines from Mrs Finnis, from Thetford, Norfolk, England. Coat, colour and texture were vastly improved by taking Clover's offspring back to her dam's side.

Her progeny included 12 American Champions. The most outstanding of her sons was Ch. Yorkboro One Step Closer ROM who was an all-breed BIS and multiple Specialty winner. His litter brother, Ch. Yorkboro Step By Step ROM, was the more valuable of the two in passing his quality traits to his get. Clover's son, Ch. Yorkboro Follow The Leader ROM, made a significant contribution to Yorkboro in his consistent passing of conformation to his offspring. Two all-breed BIS winners, Ch. Yorkboro Color By Number and Ch. Yorkboro My Main Man ROM, were Clover grandsons. My Main Man was the top-winning Yorkshire Terrier in 1991 as well as the Westminster Kennel Club BOB winner in the same year. Two outstanding Group-winning sons were: Ch. Yorkboro Puttin' On The Ritz and Ch. Yorkboro Stop The Music.

Clover's most outstanding daughters included Ch. Yorkboro Touch And Go ROM, Ch. Yorkboro All Time High ROM and Ch. Yorkboro Any Day Now ROM. These bitches were significant because they consistently passed their superior conformation traits to many of their offspring. Yorkboro has had six consecutive generations of Champion bitches descendent from Clover. All told, Clover's progeny include four BIS winners, twelve Group winners and six Specialty winners.

Clover's traits are evident today in the lines of Yorkboro (Doreen Hubbard), Elite (Carol Confer), Delshire (Deloras Maas), Whirlwind (Mark Chilcutt and Frank Larrieu) and Pastoral (Lorraine Hayes).

AM., PR, LA, INT. CH. CARANEAL'S CHARGED AND READY ROM
Born in 1988, 'Kristopher' is owner-bred and shown by Georgette and Robert Franzoni. He started his show career at the age of nine months, winning Reserve Winners Dog from the 9-12 month Puppy Class at the Delaware Valley Yorkshire Terrier Club Specialty on November 20 1988 under Osman Sameja of Ozmilion kennel fame from England.

Kristopher was also Grand Sweepstakes winner in New York in February 1989. All the points necessary to become a Champion were won from the Bred by Exhibitor Class, shown by his breeder/owner Georgette Franzoni. Kristopher was the Pedigree Award winner for 1991, 1992 and 1993, and has also won 20 Yorkshire Terrier Specialty shows and three All Breed Best in Shows. His 20 Specialty wins include four sets of back to back Specialty wins and six National

Specialty wins. Nine Specialty wins were under breeder/judges, including the 1994 Best of Breed at the Yorkshire Terrier Club of Greater New York in New York City under Osman Sameja. He was BOB at the Westminster Kennel Club show in February 1993.

Kristopher was the Top Yorkshire Terrier (All Breed) for 1993 and has sired 52 Champions to date and is still being used at stud.

AM	= American Champion
BDA	= Bermuda Champion
PR	= Puerto Rican Champion
LA	= Latin America Champion
Int. Ch.	= International Champion
ROM	= A special suffix awarded by the Yorkshire Terrier Club of America to dogs who have sired six Champions, or to bitches who are the dams of three Champions.

RESCUE AND REHOMING IN THE US

Rescue of Yorkshire Terriers from abusive homes, or from homes that no longer either want them or can care for them, is becoming a problem. Many people purchase a cute Yorkie puppy on a whim, with little preparation or insight into the breed and its characteristics.

Unfortunately, there are too many people breeding Yorkies who know very little about the breed and its temperament, and thus cannot advise prospective owners if this is really the breed of dog they should think about

Am. Ch. Caraneal's Charged And Ready ROM.

owning. While the larger size Yorkies (over 7 lbs) can successfully be raised with older children, many responsible breeders will not place their puppies with families that have young children.

The responsible breeder will not only check out the prospective owner's home situation and lifestyle, but can also advise the owner about training, housebreaking, behaviour patterns and, in some cases, even health. The 'casual' breeder is not equipped to do this and thus leaves the new owner to fend for himself in most situations.

One of the main reasons that Yorkies get placed in rescue is due to behaviorial problems: housebreaking, barking, nipping, etc. The new owner was never apprised of the nature of the Yorkie, so was never told how to cope with any problems should they arise. A responsible breeder will tell the prospective owners that training must begin from day one in the new owner's home and it must be consistent: the Yorkie cannot be reprimanded today for something he has been allowed to do before.

Some Yorkies are placed in rescue due to health problems; some of these problems the Yorkie has acquired, while others are of a hereditary nature. Some health problems are relatively easy to manage, while others are much more difficult and costly so, to some people with limited income this makes the situation prohibitive; thus the Yorkie gets placed in rescue.

The Yorkshire Terrier Club of America, Inc. has an extensive network of both members and non-members working in rescue. Mary Elizabeth Dugmore is the National Chairman for YTCA Rescue and has very recently formed a connective group known as YESS (Yorkie Express State to State) which helps to transport Yorkies from one location to another if the prospective owner of the 'rescue' lives a distance from where the dog is presently located.

The YTCA rescue team has been very successful in placing almost all of the Yorkies that they have taken in. Frequent reports indicate that the dogs adjust very rapidly and are very happy in their new homes. All dogs placed through YTCA rescue are spayed or neutered and are health-checked by a veterinarian; they are given a heartworm check, and are brought up to date on their shots if necessary, before being placed with their new owners. A donation is expected if a Yorkie is turned in to rescue, but a set fee to cover the cost of veterinary expenses is charged when a dog is placed in a new home.

SMOKY THE WAR DOG
No account of Yorkshire Terriers in America would be complete without mention of Smoky the war dog. Little 4lb Smoky was found in a foxhole in New Guinea in the Second World War and travelled throughout the South

Pacific with her adopted owner, Bill Wynne. Bill taught Smoky many tricks and she spent time entertaining the troops on New Guinea.

We call Smoky our first Yorkie rescue and Therapy dog because she also visited and entertained wounded soldiers in the New Guinea and Australian hospitals. Bill smuggled Smoky back to the US in an old gas mask container when he was returned after active duty and she shared Bill's

life thereafter with his wife and a growing family.

Upon their return to the US, Bill and Smoky made countless appearances on stage and TV, as by this time, they had a routine they regularly performed using miniature equipment which was specially made for the tiny dog. She could walk a tightrope, ride a tricycle, and weave back and forth through Bill's legs.

Smoky: The first Yorkie Rescue and Therapy dog, pictured in 1944.